WHAT IS HUMANISM FOR?

"There is no philosopher today better qualified to answer the question of what humanism is for than Richard Norman. His humanism is one with a cool head and warm heart."
Julian Baggini, writer and philosopher

"This insightful and accessible book illuminates the vital role of humanism in addressing the crisis of meaning in our troubled age."
Andrew Copson, Chief Executive of Humanists UK and President of Humanists International

"This pellucid little book can be read with pleasure by atheists and theists alike. It is well argued, nuanced and fair to all sides."
Robin Gill, Emeritus Professor of Applied Theology, University of Kent

"Crystal clear, informative and always fair-minded ... merits careful attention even from those who cannot share Norman's worldview."
John Cottingham, Professor Emeritus of Philosophy, University of Reading

"A *tour de force* introduction to humanism, one of the most significant – and most misunderstood – existential movements of the modern age."
Lois Lee, University of Kent, 'Explaining Atheism' Principal Investigator

The status quo is broken. The world is grappling with a web of challenges that could threaten our very existence. If we believe in a better world, now is the time to question the purpose behind our actions and those taken in our name.

Enter the What Is It For? series – a bold exploration of the core elements shaping our world, from religion and free speech to animal rights and war. This series cuts through the noise to reveal the true impact of these topics, what they really do and why they matter.

Ditching the usual heated debates and polarizations, this series offers fresh, forward-thinking insights. Leading experts present groundbreaking ideas and point to ways forward for real change, urging us to envision a brighter future.

Each book dives into the history and function of its subject, uncovering its role in society and, crucially, how it can be better.

Series editor: George Miller

Visit **bristoluniversitypress.co.uk/what-is-it-for** to find out more about the series.

Available now

WHAT ARE ANIMAL RIGHTS FOR?
Steve Cooke

WHAT IS COUNTERTERRORISM FOR?
Leonie Jackson

WHAT IS CYBERSECURITY FOR?
Tim Stevens

WHAT IS HISTORY FOR?
Robert Gildea

WHAT IS HUMANISM FOR?
Richard Norman

WHAT IS JOURNALISM FOR?
Jon Allsop

WHAT IS THE MONARCHY FOR?
Laura Clancy

WHAT ARE MUSEUMS FOR?
Jon Sleigh

WHAT ARE THE OLYMPICS FOR?
Jules Boykoff

WHAT IS PHILANTHROPY FOR?
Rhodri Davies

WHAT ARE PRISONS FOR?
Hindpal Singh Bhui

WHAT IS VEGANISM FOR?
Catherine Oliver

WHAT IS WAR FOR?
Jack McDonald

WHAT IS THE WELFARE STATE FOR?
Paul Spicker

WHAT ARE ZOOS FOR?
Heather Browning and Walter Veit

Forthcoming

- **WHAT IS ANARCHISM FOR?**
  Nathan Jun

- **WHAT IS ANTHROPOLOGY FOR?**
  Kriti Kapila

- **WHAT ARE CONSPIRACY THEORIES FOR?**
  James Fitzgerald

- **WHAT IS DRUG POLICY FOR?**
  Julia Buxton

- **WHAT IS FIFA FOR?**
  Alan Tomlinson

- **WHAT IS FREE SPEECH FOR?**
  Gavan Titley

- **WHAT IS IMMIGRATION POLICY FOR?**
  Madeleine Sumption

- **WHAT IS INTERNATIONAL DEVELOPMENT FOR?**
  Andrea Cornwall

- **WHAT ARE MARKETS FOR?**
  Phillip Roscoe

- **WHAT IS MUSIC FOR?**
  Fleur Brouwer

- **WHAT ARE NUCLEAR WEAPONS FOR?**
  Patricia Shamai

- **WHAT IS RELIGION FOR?**
  Malise Ruthven

- **WHAT IS RESILIENCE FOR?**
  Hamideh Mahdiani

- **WHAT IS SPACE EXPLORATION FOR?**
  Tony Milligan and Koji Tachibana

- **WHAT ARE STATUES FOR?**
  Milly Williamson

- **WHAT IS TRUTH FOR?**
  Nick Enfield

RICHARD NORMAN is Emeritus Professor of Moral Philosophy at the University of Kent, a Patron of Humanists UK and a member of Humanist Climate Action. He has published widely in the fields of ethics and political philosophy.

WHAT IS HUMANISM FOR?

RICHARD NORMAN

First published in Great Britain in 2025 by

Bristol University Press
University of Bristol
1–9 Old Park Hill
Bristol
BS2 8BB
UK
t: +44 (0)117 374 6645
e: bup-info@bristol.ac.uk

Details of international sales and distribution partners are available at
bristoluniversitypress.co.uk

© Richard Norman 2025

British Library Cataloguing in Publication Data
A catalogue record for this book is available from the British Library

ISBN 978-1-5292-4199-0 paperback
ISBN 978-1-5292-4200-3 ePub
ISBN 978-1-5292-4201-0 ePdf

The right of Richard Norman to be identified as author of this work has been
asserted by him in accordance with the Copyright, Designs and Patents Act 1988.

All rights reserved: no part of this publication may be reproduced, stored in
a retrieval system, or transmitted in any form or by any means, electronic,
mechanical, photocopying, recording, or otherwise without the prior permission of
Bristol University Press.

Every reasonable effort has been made to obtain permission to reproduce
copyrighted material. If, however, anyone knows of an oversight, please contact
the publisher.

The statements and opinions contained within this publication are solely those
of the author and not of the University of Bristol or Bristol University Press.
The University of Bristol and Bristol University Press disclaim responsibility for
any injury to persons or property resulting from any material published in this
publication.

Bristol University Press works to counter discrimination on grounds of gender,
race, disability, age and sexuality.

Cover design: Tom Appshaw

Bristol University Press' authorised representative in the European
Union is: Easy Access System Europe, Mustamäe tee 50, 10621
Tallinn, Estonia, Email: gpsr.requests@easproject.com

CONTENTS

List of Figures		x
Acknowledgements		xiii
1	**Making Sense**	**1**
2	**Beliefs**	**27**
3	**Meaning**	**48**
4	**Values**	**67**
5	**Community**	**89**
6	**Politics**	**104**
7	**Conclusion**	**126**
Notes		**139**
Further Reading		**145**
Index		**149**

LIST OF FIGURES

1.1 Changes in religion and belief in Britain over a 40-year period. (Graph by Jeremy Rodell, Humanists UK, drawing on data from NatCen Social Research [2024] *British Social Attitudes Survey* [data series], *4th Release*, UK Data Service. SN: 200006, DOI: http://doi.org/10.5255/UKDA-Series-200006.) 7

1.2 Religious 'nones' in America (2007–23). (Source: Pew Research Center. 2020–23 data based on Pew Research Center's National Public Opinion Reference Surveys, nationally representative surveys conducted online and by mail, respondents recruited using address-based sampling. Data from 2019 and earlier comes from the Center's random-digit-dial phone surveys, including the 2007 and 2014 Religious Landscape Studies.) 7

1.3 George Eliot (1819–80) by the Swiss artist Alexandre-Louis-François d'Albert-Durade (1804–86). (National Portrait Gallery, London, public domain.) 23

2.1 White marble bust of Epicurus. (British Museum, London. Photograph by Marie-Lan Nguyen, released into the public domain by the copyright holder.) 44

LIST OF FIGURES

3.1	A humanist funeral. (Photograph reproduced by permission of Sue Baumbach, Humanists UK Accredited Celebrant.)	63
4.1	Erich Fromm (1900–80). (Photograph by Müller-May. Public domain.)	73
4.2	Margaret K. Knight (1903–83). (Photograph reproduced by permission of Conway Hall Humanist Library and Archives.)	79
5.1	Conway Hall, in Red Lion Square, London. (By geni, 2019. Reproduced under CC BY-SA 4.0 licence.)	93
5.2	A humanist wedding ceremony. (Reproduced by permission of Humanists UK.)	96
6.1	Thomas Paine. (Engraving by William Sharp after a painting by George Romney. LC-DIG-ppmsca-24327, Library of Congress Prints & Photographs Division Washington, DC. Public domain.)	108
6.2	Mary Wollstonecraft. (Photograph [from 1850 to 1870] of a stipple engraving by James Heath, c. 1797, after a painting by John Opie. Reference number LC-USZ62-64309, Library of Congress Prints & Photographs Division Washington, DC. Public domain.)	108
6.3	The Peterloo Massacre, engraving by Richard Carlile. (Manchester Libraries. © National Portrait Gallery, London.)	113
6.4	John Stuart Mill, steel engraving, 1866. (Public domain.)	117

7.1 Bertrand Russell. (Photograph by Underwood & Underwood. LC-USZ62-49535, Library of Congress Prints & Photographs Division Washington, DC. Public domain.)   131

ACKNOWLEDGEMENTS

I am grateful to George Miller, for his guidance through all the stages of planning and writing this book; to Lynne Broadbent, for reading an earlier draft and providing valuable feedback; and to the many school pupils, of all ages, to whom I have given talks over the years, and who have helped me to clarify my thoughts about what humanism is and what it is for.

1
MAKING SENSE

Why do we need humanism? What is it for? This is a serious question, and I intend to take it seriously. I begin therefore with some brief general reflections on the nature of human needs. What do people live by? What do we need in order to function effectively as human beings?

A frame of orientation and devotion

The answer begins, of course, with physical needs – the need for food and drink, for shelter and protection from the elements, and for physical health, the proper functioning of our organs and limbs. These are needs which we share with many other biological species.

However, there are other needs which derive from our distinctive nature as human beings. These we might describe as psychological needs, or perhaps as 'existential needs'. Human beings, unlike most – and probably all – other animals, cannot simply live instinctively, from day to day and moment to moment. We are condemned to *think*. We have to make *decisions*. We cannot escape the need to try to understand the world around us, to find our way around in it, to predict what will happen if we act in this way or that. And we cannot be motivated just by instinctive desires, we cannot avoid thinking about what we want, whether we prefer this or that, and how best to get what we want. In short, we have to try to make sense of our world and our lives.

Some might say that we think too much, that we should try to get back in touch with our animal instincts, act on our 'gut feelings' and resist the tendency to over-intellectualize. In crisis situations we do indeed act instinctively to defend ourselves, to react to danger and fight to survive. But as a general recommendation for how to live, the call to 'trust your instincts' is itself, of course, a product of the intellect. Various writers have from time to time made a case for it, decrying the over-civilized and artificial way of life of their society, but the case which they make for living more 'instinctively' is one which they have to argue for, to construct with reasons. And the attempt to live by it would itself be a consciously adopted policy, requiring us constantly to remind ourselves to 'stop thinking'!

In short, a fundamental human need is the need for what the American humanist Erich Fromm called *a frame of orientation and devotion*. His explanation of this phrase, in his many writings, was based on a view of what makes us distinctively human. This is how he put it (writing at a time when the word 'man' was still used to refer to all of humanity):

> Man's capacity for self-awareness, reason, and imagination – new qualities that go beyond the capacity for instrumental thinking of even the cleverest animals – requires a picture of the world and of his place in it that is structured and has inner cohesion. Man needs a map of his natural and social world, without which he would be confused and unable to act purposefully and consistently. He would have no way of orienting himself and of finding for himself a fixed point that permits him to organize all the impressions that impinge upon him ...
>
> But a map is not enough as a guide for action; man also needs a goal that tells him where to go. The animal has no such problems. Its instincts provide it ... with goals. But man, lacking instinctive determination and having a brain that permits him to think of many directions in which he could go, needs ... an object of devotion to be the focal point of all his strivings and the basis for all his ... values. The objects of man's devotion vary. He can be devoted to an idol which requires him to kill his children or to an ideal that makes him protect children; he can be devoted to the growth of life or to its destruction ... He can be devoted to the most diverse goals and idols; yet while the difference in the objects of devotion are [sic] of immense importance, the need for devotion itself is a primary existential need.[1]

Again, it might be objected that this over-intellectualizes the human situation. Granted, it may be said, we cannot avoid having to think, but most of us are not thinkers. We often have to decide what to do, but do we all need an overall philosophy of life? Why do our beliefs about the world have to be a comprehensive 'map', a system with 'inner cohesion'? And why do our innumerable particular goals have to be focused on an 'object of devotion'? It may be true that we cannot live entirely by our instincts, but don't most people live largely from day to day, and manage perfectly well in the process?

The inescapable need for at least some degree of cohesion is most apparent at the practical level. People sometimes find that their desires and goals conflict, and they cannot help having to reflect on what is most important to them. Is there more to life than the accumulation of wealth and material possessions? How do we deal with dilemmas about sexuality, gender roles and identities? Does it matter that we are destroying the natural environment for future generations? Their answers will in turn depend on at least a rough and ready set of beliefs about what the world is like. They will believe either that this life is the only one we have, or that how we live now will have consequences for a possible life after death, for what there might be to come in a 'heaven' or 'hell' or a future incarnation. They will believe either that there is some non-human source of guidance about what we should live for, or that we have to think for ourselves using simply the accumulated reasoning of our fellow human beings. They will believe either that our future lies in our hands, or that there is some non-human purpose or fate or destiny which will determine how things turn out.

People need a way of thinking about these questions. They need a framework of values and beliefs. Most people have at least implicit values and beliefs of a general kind, but these will not guide us to act wisely unless we try to examine them and think about them in a more thoroughgoing way. Humanism, I will suggest, is a response to that need.

Humanism, religion and secularization

The need for a frame of orientation and devotion is one which has historically been met by the world's religions. All past societies seem to have had a religion of some kind. Religions have varied enormously, but they have typically provided a set of beliefs about what the world is like and our place in it. They have embodied a view on whether our day-to-day world is the only reality there is or whether there is also some other realm of existence, and have typically tended towards the latter. They have always furnished guidance about how people should live their lives, ranging from a general ethical imperative to 'love your neighbour' or 'be compassionate' to a body of sometimes extremely detailed rules governing every aspect of life.

However, to varying degrees in different parts of the world, organized religions no longer command the support they once did. The British Social Attitudes (BSA) survey of 2019 highlighted the changes in Britain. It noted that the decline in religious practice and affiliation is a long-term trend:

> In Britain, church attendance has declined steadily since at least 1851, when a government count showed about half the population in church on a particular Sunday. The figure derived from recent clergy counts is around 6%. In 1900 church membership was around 25%; it is now less than 10%. In 1900 more than half the age-relevant population attended Sunday schools; now it is less than 4%. Similar declines are visible in the use of religious offices to mark rites of passage. In the nineteenth century, around 90% of Scottish weddings were religious; in 2017 the figure was 30% and in 2012 there were more humanist than Catholic weddings. Before the Second World War, the Church of England was baptising three-quarters of the English population; the figure now is 15%.[2]

In the more recent period since 1983, when the BSA surveys began, the changes have been striking. In 1983, 66 per cent of the British population identified as Christian. By 2018, the proportion had fallen to 38 per cent, while 52 per cent said that they do not regard themselves as belonging to any religion.[3] The proportion of the population belonging to non-Christian faiths slowly increased over that period but remained below 10 per cent, with Muslims making up about 5 per cent or 6 per cent of the population.

The details of these changes are debated, as are the various possible explanations. The underlying causes of religious decline which can plausibly be cited include industrialization, urbanization, increased geographical and social mobility and the decline of close-knit rural communities; greater cultural diversity, the

Figure 1.1: Changes in religion and belief in Britain over a 40-year period

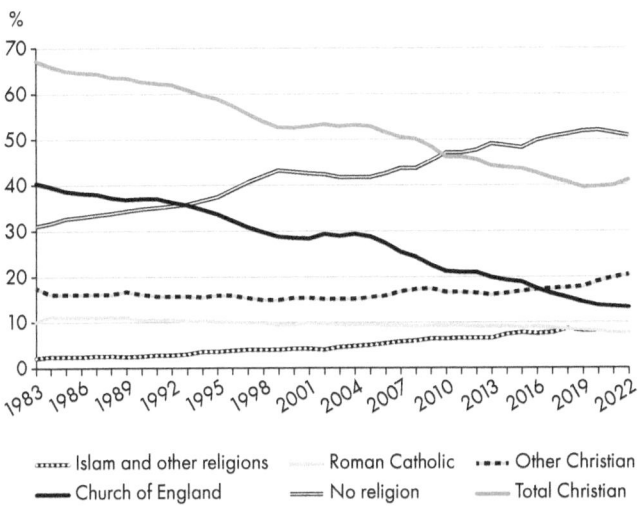

Figure 1.2: Religious 'nones' in America (2007–23)

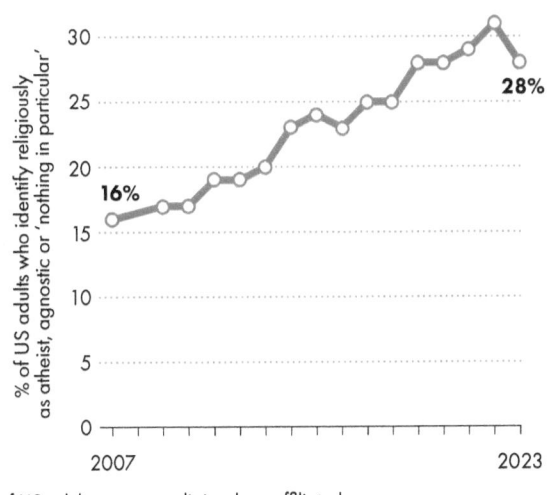

28% of US adults are now religiously unaffiliated.

trend towards individualism and the questioning of authority; the growth of literacy and education, making it easier for people to decide on their own beliefs; and the changing role of women, increasingly working outside the home whereas they had in the past been the main transmitters of traditional beliefs and values within the family. No doubt all these factors have played a role and have interacted. The most striking feature throwing light on the changes is the decline in the extent to which religious parents pass on their religion to their children. As the BSA report puts it, the changes have happened not primarily because adults have been losing their faith, but because:

> religious decline in Britain is generational; people tend to be less religious than their parents, and on average their children are even less religious than they are. Two non-religious parents successfully transmit their lack of religion. Two religious parents have roughly a 50/50 chance of passing on the faith. One religious parent does only half as well as two together.[4]

In short, people increasingly make their own decisions about what they believe, rather than inherit a pre-packaged set of doctrines and practices from their family and their community.

The pattern in Britain is largely mirrored in other Western European societies. The United States is often claimed to be significantly different, and to be a society in which religion plays a more powerful part, but in fact, although the numbers are different, the overall trajectory is similar. A 2021 report by the Pew Research Centre found that, although Christians continue to be in the majority, the proportion of the population identifying as Christian decreased from 75 per cent in 2011 to 63 per cent in 2021. When asked about their religious affiliation, 29 per cent of American adults described themselves as atheists, agnostics, or 'nothing in particular'.[5]

The trend described here is often referred to as 'secularization'.[6] If we use that term, it is important to be clear about what is and what is not being claimed. In the societies referred to, and other similar societies elsewhere in Europe and in countries such as Canada, Australia and New Zealand where Christianity was previously the dominant religion, the secularization process is undeniably a long-term one, which at present shows no sign of going into reverse. That is not to say that it is a uniform process. There may be particular religious revivals of one sort or another, such as the emergence of new evangelical churches which challenge the dominance of the established Church. There are, of course, significant minorities adhering to non-Christian religions, in particular Islam and Hinduism, largely in consequence of population movement. But as the BSA data and census data show, the overall tendency is clear.

Reference to the process of secularization does not necessarily involve a claim that this process is irreversible. Although there is as yet no evidence of a reversal, it would be folly to make sweeping predictions. But what does seem plausible, as already indicated, is that secularization is itself a reflection of more fundamental social changes which are themselves likely to continue. It is not some kind of intellectual conversion which could be countered simply by more effective persuasion and proselytizing.

As I have said, the process is also not a universal one. It is specific to particular parts of the modern world. There are, of course, societies which are intensely religious, and where the dominant religion is held in place by political authority and social pressure. There are societies such as some African countries, in particular, where Christianity and Islam are in intense competition, both of them supported by lavish financial backing from elsewhere, and sometimes existing alongside indigenous religions. How these phenomena will play out is impossible to know.

Confining ourselves, then, to what we know, we can see the beginning of an answer to the question 'What is humanism for?'. In a world where traditional religions are no longer meeting many people's need for a 'frame of orientation and devotion', humanism is an alternative approach to meeting that need, an approach which is, in a sense to be defined, non-religious.

A non-religious worldview

But why, you might ask, is any such alternative needed? If people are moving away from organized systems of belief, if the decline of institutionalized religion means that individuals are making their own choices and decisions about their own personal beliefs and values, then why seek to offer them an alternative non-religious belief system? Why not simply leave it to individuals to make their pick-and-mix choices from a seemingly limitless array of options?

This is where we have to emphasize the word 'frame'.[7] Humanism, as we shall see, is not a set of doctrines. It is not a creed. It is not a prescribed body of practices or a code of moral rules. It is a *framework*, a way of thinking and living, a broad approach within which we can locate our innumerable more specific beliefs and grapple with our particular practical dilemmas and challenges. It is what is sometimes also called a 'worldview', and that term again emphasizes its nature as an overall perspective, a way of seeing our world and our place in it. It is broad and general, but it is not vague or empty. It draws on a long tradition of thinking outside the limits of organized religion, a tradition which has sometimes had to fight its way against imposed or established orthodoxy and has, in the process, progressively shaped a vision of how to live without religion.

In what sense, then, is humanism a distinctively 'non-religious' worldview? A simple answer would be that it does not involve any belief in a god or gods, or supernatural beings – but that would be *too* simple. Not all religions are theistic. Buddhism and Taoism, for instance, or at least important strands in those traditions, do not include belief in a god. And within theistic religions, how the concept of 'god' is understood varies enormously. At one extreme it can be a highly personalized idea of a superhuman being who watches over us and guides our actions, and with whom we can hold conversations. At the other extreme it may be interpreted as a very abstract idea such as 'the ground of being' or 'ultimate concern' – so abstract as to make it unclear what would or would not count as belief in God. In general, the great diversity of religions has to be acknowledged, as a caution against too simplistic a definition of humanism as a rejection of religion. Religions have been, as far as we know, a feature of every historical society, and their variability is as wide as the variability of human cultures. Defining humanism as a non-religious worldview, then, though correct, does not take us very far.

One important feature of humanism which differentiates it from a typically religious perspective is the rejection of any appeal to revealed truth. Whereas religions, at least in literate societies, are likely to have their own sacred texts to whose authority they appeal, at the heart of humanism is the emphasis on the use of independent critical judgement based on human experience and human reason. Again, religious believers vary greatly in this respect. Some treat their holy book as the direct word of God, to be understood literally and applied in every detail to life in the modern world. Others recognize that these texts, however inspired, are human creations reflecting the attitudes and assumptions of the culture within which they were written, and need to be interpreted to ascertain their meaning and relevance for the contemporary believer. Moreover, it would be entirely implausible and unjust to claim that the reliance on reason is the prerogative of the humanist tradition. Even extreme textual literalists appeal to the logical ingenuity of scholars to determine the practical application of their texts. Great religious thinkers such as Maimonides, Aquinas and Averroes, drawing on the philosophers of the ancient Greek world, engaged in highly sophisticated rational argument and enquiry about the beliefs of their faith tradition, as have their modern successors. The fact remains that the great thinkers and the typical ordinary religious person alike regularly exhibit the need to invoke their scriptures in order to authenticate their beliefs and assertions.

Here too, however, we have to be cautious about claiming too stark a contrast between the humanist and the religious approach. I have said that humanism emphasizes the paramount importance of rational enquiry employing independent critical judgement. But, of course, none of our beliefs could have been arrived at simply by using our own unaided individual reason. From birth onwards our view of the world is derived from our parents and carers, and though we may come to criticize and reject parts of it, we continue to depend on shared experience, the testimony of others, and the authority of experts. Humanism, as we shall see, places great value on scientific knowledge, in particular, but most of us are not scientists; we necessarily take a great deal on trust, and scientists themselves work within a collaborative scientific community and build on theories which they inherit from others.

It is therefore imperative that humanism should be able to give an account of 'rational trust' which distinguishes it from uncritical appeal to authority. In the case of our reliance on the sciences, in particular, we need some understanding of the nature of scientific method, the use which practising scientists make of observation and experiment, the rigorous testing of hypotheses, the nature of scientific institutions whose procedures promote mutual criticism and peer review, and the practical applications of scientific theories. Our constant use of modern technologies in our daily lives is a continual confirmation of the success of scientific enquiry.

Perhaps the best way to characterize the humanist commitment to independent critical thought is to look at the historical tradition which exemplifies it and from which it emerges. Modern humanism is an international movement, but it began as a European phenomenon. My brief survey will focus largely on its development in Europe and, in particular, in Britain.

The historical tradition

Like so much else in European thought and culture, important strands in the historical tradition which leads to modern humanism can be traced back to ancient Greece – to the world of the many independent city-states flourishing in mainland Greece, the Aegean islands and the coast of what is now Turkey in the 6th and 5th centuries BCE. What we find in early Greek thinkers of this period is the emergence of a *naturalistic* view of the world – an approach to explaining the nature of the universe and the changes we observe in it by reference to purely physical causes. This was in contrast to traditional ideas that all sorts of events could be explained by the intervention of the gods in human affairs – that disasters such as diseases and storms, a shipwreck or a bad harvest occurred because the gods were angry with humans, or that good fortune such as a fair wind for a voyage was sent by a god or goddess to assist their favourite mortal.

The philosopher Empedocles, for example, writing in the middle of the 5th century BCE, put forward the idea that everything that exists is made up of the same physical constituents, the four underlying elements of earth, water, air and fire. All the features of our world, including the existence of living things, and the changes which take place in the world, can be explained by the physical combining and recombining of these four elements in innumerable different ways. For Leucippus and Democritus, writing a little later, the underlying components of the universe are not Empedocles' four elements but an infinite number of invisibly small particles which they called 'atoms'. The huge variety of ways in which these atoms can be arranged, by purely natural processes of colliding, cohering and separating, can, they said, account for everything that exists and all the changes which we see taking place in the world. These striking anticipations of modern scientific concepts are not themselves science – they were not tested with rigorous controlled experiments – but they represent the use of bold critical thought, backed by everyday observations, to construct an essentially naturalistic framework with which to understand the world.

The naturalistic world view of these early Greek thinkers was taken further, in the 4th century BCE, by Epicurus. He took over the atomic theory and promoted it with the principal aim of banishing fear from human life. Understanding the true causes of physical phenomena, he said, relieves us of the fears of divine intervention. And since we humans are ourselves made up of physical atoms, we have no immaterial and immortal soul which could experience punishments in a world to come. Hence, he said, there is no need for us to fear death. The good life is the enjoyment of this life, a life of simple pleasures and freedom from pain and fear. Values such as justice and friendship contribute to human pleasure by enabling us to live harmoniously with one another. The Epicurean philosophy later became popular in the Roman world, and the exposition of it in the great poem *On the Nature of Things* by the Roman poet Lucretius in the 1st century BCE was one of the principal means by which Epicureanism was preserved and rediscovered in modern Europe.

When modern humanists look to the ancient world, then, for the beginnings of a humanist tradition, they focus especially on this commitment to critical enquiry and a willingness to challenge traditional beliefs and accepted religious ideas, the development of naturalism as a framework for understanding the world around us, and the grounding of ethical values in human needs and human experience.

Strikingly similar ideas were to be found in Indian thought. A group of thinkers more or less contemporary with the early Greek philosophers were the Chavarkas, also known as the Lokayata. They rejected the mainstream tendency of Indian thought and the authority of the Vedas, the earliest sacred texts of Hinduism, and we know of them only from the reports of their critics, but they appear to have defended a thoroughgoing naturalism. The only reality, they said, is the world perceived by the senses. Like Empedocles, they explained all the components of this world as being composed of the four elements, earth, water, air and fire. Supposedly non-physical items such as intelligence were in fact the product of these physical elements 'in the same way in which red colour is produced from the combination of betel, areca nut and lime'.[8] The self ('atman') is nothing over and beyond the body. We do not survive the death of the body, and there is no heaven and no hell for us to experience after death. The only heaven is that of worldly pleasures, and the only hell is the pain inflicted on us by other human beings, and by diseases and other causes of suffering. And 'moksa', the state of enlightenment and liberation pursued by orthodox Hindu teachings, is to be found simply in the peace of death.

It is not known whether there was any influence either way between the thinkers of ancient Greece and of ancient India, but certainly the former came to be seen as important forerunners of modern European humanism, and as humanism became an international movement it was enriched by the discovery of continuities with earlier ideas from many different cultures. Here, then, we have examples which illustrate clearly what is meant by the tradition of critical enquiry from which humanism derives.

Turning then to the emergence of modern humanism, we find that 'humanist' and 'humanism' were not initially the words that were used. The original use of the word 'humanist' referred to those scholars in Renaissance Italy and elsewhere who rediscovered and studied the texts of the ancient world, especially after the fall of Constantinople to the Ottoman empire in 1453. The Renaissance humanists thereby contributed to an important resource for modern humanism but were not 'humanists' in the modern sense. The thinkers we are looking at in the humanist tradition were variously called, and called themselves, 'free-thinkers' and 'deists', and later 'secularists' and 'rationalists', and the word 'humanist' only came to the fore in the 20th century. This tradition is not, therefore, unified by a single label. Rather, it is a tradition which, to varying degrees, criticized received and established religion, in ways which may in some cases appear mild now but were in their time bold and radical, and offered alternative ways of thinking and living.

In the 18th century it was associated especially with what has come to be known as the European Enlightenment. To have openly rejected all religious beliefs would have been highly dangerous, so we do not know to what extent to take their professed views at face value. Some espoused 'deism', a position popularized by Thomas Paine (1737–1809) in his book *The Age of Reason*. Deists accepted the case for a divine creator but distinguished this from the adherence to organized

Christianity and its creeds and rituals. Voltaire (1694–1778), for example, was a deist; he rejected atheism, but his famous work *Candide* was a scathing satirical attack on belief in a divine providence which guarantees that this is 'the best of all possible worlds' despite all the evidence of suffering. The Scottish philosopher David Hume (1711–76) was the great philosophical sceptic, and his essay on miracles was a masterly logical demonstration that the balance of probabilities will always make any belief in miracles untenable. He was also a master of irony, and used it in his *Dialogues concerning Natural Religion*, published posthumously, to undermine all arguments for the existence of a deity, without explicitly avowing that conclusion.

The most radical of these Enlightenment thinkers was Baron d'Holbach (1723–89), who was born in Germany but spent most of his life in Paris. He defended a thoroughgoing naturalism, arguing that everything that exists is a part of nature. Human beings too are material beings, subject to the laws of nature, and it is only by coming to understand nature and its laws that we can achieve happiness. The idea of an immaterial substance, such as the soul or God, can be given no intelligible meaning.

He recognized rather cautiously that this led to atheism, and it is unsurprising that his most important book *The System of Nature* was published under a pseudonym.

These Enlightenment thinkers were, in their time, outliers in their opposition to conventionally accepted religious views. In the 19th century, religious doubts became more widespread. It is sometimes supposed that the 'crisis of faith' was triggered by the publication in 1859 of Darwin's *Origin of Species*, but the picture is more complicated than that. An important earlier shift was the emerging view of how the Bible should be read, and the growing recognition that a critical reading was as appropriate to this as to any other ancient texts. A landmark in this debate was the publication by the German scholar David Friedrich Strauss in 1835 of his *The Life of Jesus Critically Examined*. Strauss's starting point was the increasing conflict between, on the one hand, the view of religious records as 'sacred history', 'a history of events in which the divine enters, without intermediation, into the human', and, on the other, the growing acceptance of a view of the world as 'a chain of causes and effects connecting natural phenomena with each other'.[9] The conflict is driven, then, by the increasing acceptance of the scientific worldview in general rather than by any specific scientific discovery. Strauss proposed that a distinction had to be made between what in the Bible is 'myth' and what is history, and the criterion for making this distinction is whether 'the narration is irreconcilable with the known and universal laws which govern the course of events':

> When therefore we meet with an account of certain phenomena or events of which it is either expressly stated or implied that they were produced immediately by God himself (divine apparitions – voices from heaven and the like), or by human beings possessed of supernatural

powers (miracles, prophecies), such an account is *in so far* to be considered as not historical.[10] (emphasis in original)

The radical implication of this approach is that key elements of the life of Jesus as narrated in the Gospels, such as the Virgin Birth, miracles and the Resurrection, cannot be viewed as historical events.

This new way of thinking about the Bible and the historical Jesus had an enormous impact. For some, it could be consistent with a 'liberal' Christianity, but for others it led to a radical loss of their Christian faith. The best-selling novel by Mrs Humphry Ward, *Robert Elsmere*, which sold nearly a quarter of a million copies within a few months of its publication in 1888, and clearly struck a chord with many readers, portrayed a clergyman who loses his faith when he finds that he cannot answer the case for a critical approach to the reading of the Scriptures.

Another consideration pushing people in the same direction was the new understanding of the timescale of the Earth's history. Charles Lyell (1797–1875), applying a scientific approach to the study of geology, showed that all the features of the Earth's surface, far from having been laid down for all time at the Creation, could be best explained as the result of entirely natural processes operating over billions of years. This in turn provided the framework for Darwin's theory of evolution by natural selection, showing that the emergence of new species from the simplest forms of living things could likewise be explained in terms of small changes accumulating over a vast period of time. *The Origin of Species* did not therefore, when it was published in 1859, come as the huge shock which it is sometimes thought to have been. For many Christians, it was fairly readily taken on board. But, for others, it was a further contribution to the 'crisis of faith' exemplified by Matthew Arnold's famous poem 'Dover Beach', published in 1867.

> The Sea of Faith
> Was once, too, at the full, and round earth's shore
> Lay like the folds of a bright girdle furled.
> But now I only hear
> Its melancholy, long, withdrawing roar ...

Strauss's *Life of Jesus* was translated into English by Mary Ann Evans, better known as the great novelist George Eliot. She also translated another influential work, by Ludwig Feuerbach, who was, like Strauss, one of the group of German thinkers influenced by the philosopher G.W.F. Hegel and referred to as the 'Left-Hegelians' or 'Young Hegelians'. Feuerbach argued, in *The Essence of Christianity* (1841), that the Christian God is a projection of human qualities, those characteristics which define the human essence, and particularly the quality of human love. Though the term 'humanism' would seem to be singularly appropriate to describe Feuerbach's approach, he did not use such a word, but it was used in that way by other Young Hegelians including Arnold Ruge and the young Karl Marx.[11]

Other terms were coming to the fore. T.H. Huxley, the biologist who described himself as 'Darwin's

Figure 1.3: George Eliot (1819–80), by the Swiss artist Alexandre-Louis-François d'Albert-Durade (1804–86)

The great English novelist George Eliot (Mary Ann Evans) was an exemplary figure in the spread of humanist ideas in 19th-century Britain. In her youth she was a fervent evangelical Christian but then reacted strongly against it. She made friends in radical and free-thinking circles, and was persuaded to translate into English two major works of German sceptical thought, David Friedrich Strauss's *The Life of Jesus* and Ludwig Feuerbach's *The Essence of Christianity*. Her translation of these two books places her at the heart of the nineteenth-century rejection of traditional Christianity. Several years later, in a letter to friends in 1859, she wrote:

> I have no longer any antagonism towards any faith in which human sorrow and human longing for purity have expressed themselves ... I have not returned to dogmatic Christianity ... [but] my most rooted conviction is, that the immediate object and the proper sphere of all our highest emotions are our struggling fellow-men and this earthly existence.

Bulldog', employed the word 'agnosticism' for a refusal to accept beliefs about the world which could not be adequately supported by scientific evidence. The word 'secularism' was coined by George Holyoake to denote 'a code of duty pertaining to this life, founded on considerations purely human, and intended mainly for those who find theology indefinite or inadequate, unreliable or unbelievable'.[12] Secular societies were formed in the 1850s and 1860s, and in 1866 the

National Secular Society was established, with Charles Bradlaugh as its first president.

The last quarter of the 19th century saw the emergence of the 'ethical movement'. Groups calling themselves 'ethical societies' were founded by people looking for alternatives to churches and conventional religious institutions, and aimed especially at promoting moral education independent of any religious foundation. The first of these, in the United States, was the Society for Ethical Culture established by Felix Adler in New York in 1876. The creation of ethical societies gathered pace on both sides of the Atlantic, and in Chapter 5, I shall look further at the activities of the ethical societies in Britain. In 1893 the four existing societies in the United States unified under an umbrella organization, the American Ethical Union. In Britain, a Union of Ethical Societies was formed in 1896, and in 1920 it changed its name to the Ethical Union. And at a congress in Zurich in 1896, ethical societies from the United States, Britain, Germany, Austria, Switzerland and France united themselves in the International Ethical Union.

It was in the first half of the 20th century that the use of the words 'humanist' and 'humanism' increasingly came to be debated as alternatives to other terminology – a debate in which a clear distinction was not always made between substantive questions about what to believe and pragmatic questions about the best word to use.[13] In 1967 the Ethical Union became the British Humanist Association, changing its name in 2017 to Humanists UK. Internationally, the International Ethical Union had ceased to exist when the Second World War broke out, but in 1952 a new international body was set up, prompted in part by the experience of the war, of Nazism and Fascism and the terrible violations of fundamental human values. The International Humanist and Ethical Union (IHEU) was founded at a congress in Amsterdam by representatives from the United States, Britain, Austria, the Netherlands, Belgium, and India. Since then, it has spread beyond Europe, North America and India to become more truly global, and with that has come a greater awareness of the humanist roots to be found in non-European traditions of thought. In 2019 IHEU changed its name to Humanists International.

From this brief historical survey, it will be apparent that there is no simple definition of humanism, nor even agreement on the name. It is best defined by that history – a tradition of critical enquiry and a search for beliefs and values which will stand up to criticism, without any appeal to supposedly revealed truths from a non-human origin, and without the vulnerabilities and implausibilities of established religions.

I have traced that history to the modern humanist movement. But humanism is not confined to or defined by institutions. You do not have to be a member of a humanist organization to be a humanist. In the following chapters I shall set out my own understanding of how humanism can best be interpreted, and how it can best serve the purpose of furnishing a 'frame of orientation and devotion'. Expanding on the various strands which we have found in the humanist tradition, Chapter 2 will offer a further elucidation of what is meant by 'naturalism' as a framework for understanding the world, and Chapters 3 and 4 will consider how humanism aims to give values a naturalistic foundation, basing them on human experience and human nature. Chapter 5 will build further on the account of how the early humanist movement, including the ethical societies, responded to the declining appeal of religious communities and, in particular, of the Christian churches. And Chapter 6 will look at how the commitment to critical enquiry has political implications, such as the defence of human rights and freedom of belief and expression.

2
BELIEFS

People need beliefs. That is one aspect of the need for a frame of orientation and devotion. It does not have to take the form of a creed, a set of detailed beliefs to which we must subscribe. It is an overall perspective, a way of seeing the world and our place in it. In tracing the tradition of thought on which modern humanism draws, I have referred frequently to the stance of 'naturalism', and that, for humanism, is the framework within which our particular beliefs have their place.

Naturalism

What is naturalism? Put simply, it is the belief that this world is the only world there is. And by 'this world' is meant, equally simply, the world in which we live and with which we interact through sensory experience and physical action. Our view of the world is built up, from birth, by our interactions with other people, and by the behaviour we learn from them which enables us to find our way around and to manipulate things. We learn that we live in a world in which there are other human beings with bodies like our own, that there is the ground on which we walk and the air that we breathe and the sky above us, that there are other living things with which we share this world. This is the obvious commonsense starting point for naturalism.

In maintaining that this world is the one and only world that there is, then, naturalism is a rejection of the idea of a 'supernatural world', a 'separate plane of being' or 'different dimension of existence'. These are vague ideas, and we shall need to spell out more precisely what it is that naturalism rules out. But for the time being, this is our intuitive starting point.

The word 'naturalism' is sometimes equated with 'materialism' or 'physicalism' and at one level it is harmless enough to use those terms as synonyms. 'Physicalism' derives from the word '*physis*', which is simply the Greek equivalent of the Latin word '*natura*', from which 'naturalism' is derived. The use of the terms 'materialism' and 'physicalism' tends, however, to be tied to a particular view of the physical sciences and their place in our understanding of the world, and some caution is needed here.

The case for naturalism rests in part on the success of the natural sciences in explaining natural phenomena without any need to invoke interventions from a non-natural world. We saw in the previous chapter that a central strand in the humanist tradition has been the attempt to understand and explain the world on the basis of reason and evidence. The early Greek thinkers offered plausible ways to explain the changes in and nature of the world around us in purely natural terms, as the movements of atoms or the combining of elements. These were fertile conceptual frameworks but stopped short of detailed explanations and theories. Since then, it is thanks to the so-called 'scientific revolution' and to the steady progress in the advance of the sciences that we have come to understand the origins of our earth and its relationship to a universe vastly greater than was previously supposed, with our planet not at its centre but just one small planet revolving round one of billions of stars in one of billions of galaxies. Thanks to the advances in geology in the early 19th century, we know how our earth, with its mountains, rocks, soils, rivers and valleys, has been formed by gradual physical processes over billions of years. And in that context, we can explain scientifically the origins of living things and the emergence of species of plants and animals through the gradual process of evolution and natural selection, an understanding now securely underpinned by modern genetic theory.

The success of the natural sciences is not a knock-down case for naturalism. It does not rule out the existence of another, non-natural mode of existence, but it has made it increasingly unnecessary to invoke interventions from another domain, such as divine agency, in order to explain the natural world. The appeal to such intrusions has come to seem increasingly incongruous, puzzling rather than explanatory.

Though humanism is a form of naturalism, however, and though it sets great store on the knowledge derived from the natural sciences, it is not *reductionist*. It is not tied to the claim that the sciences are our only source of understanding. The natural world is also the human world, containing all the richness of human experience, the life of the emotions and the imagination. In seeking to understand the world, humanism appeals not only to the sciences but to the whole store of culturally shared experience. That experience is articulated not only by our everyday discourse but also and especially through the creative arts and the understanding which they furnish of ourselves and our fellow human beings. In seeking to do justice to our deepest feelings and experiences, people sometimes resort to the language of 'spirituality'. We shall look shortly at the connotations and associations of that word, and whether it is the best language for what we need to say. But certainly humanism, in espousing naturalism, is not condemned to be shallow.

The charge of reductionism is worth looking at more closely, and on examination it is not at all clear what it amounts to. The term implies that there is a single form of discourse, one privileged theoretical language which serves to identify the fundamental constituents of reality, and that other descriptions and explanations of things are either illusory or can be translated into the preferred discourse. But what is it that everything else is supposed to be 'reduced' to? The ancient Greek atomists asserted that 'all that there is' consists of 'atoms' and the 'void' in which the atoms move, and were then faced with the challenge of how the innumerable other things we want to say about the world, including the everyday language in which we describe our thoughts and actions, are supposed to be 'translated into' the language of atoms and the void. With the impressive success of Newtonian physics in the 17th century, it was sometimes supposed that all explanations could be reduced to those of mechanics, and that living things in particular could be understood as complicated machines. More recently the success of evolutionary theory has encouraged some to extend its boundaries and to put forward evolutionary psychology as the key to the understanding of human instincts and motivations. Progress in neurophysiology, unlocking the way in which the central nervous system functions through the transmission of electric signals between neurones, has led some to suppose that human psychology can be reduced to the study of brain structures and brain processes. And perhaps computer science is now the leading contender for a reductionist approach to human thought and action.

The fact is that there is no one science which can serve as a plausible candidate for a 'theory of everything', or even as a key to the understanding of human behaviour. There is no one explanatory scheme to which everything can be 'reduced'. There are multiple scientific programmes built around those theoretical concepts which have been found to be appropriate for the understanding of a particular range of phenomena. The fashionable sciences mentioned previously undoubtedly have their application. Drawing on the approach of evolutionary psychology, irrational forms of behaviour which we struggle to understand may become intelligible when we recognize that they are driven by deep-rooted instincts which once conferred a selective advantage in the struggle for survival of our early human ancestors. Neuroscience may be the right tool with which to explain a great deal of non-intentional human behaviour, such as patterns of sleep, for instance, or perhaps drug addiction, or certain forms of mental illness. But by the same token, what is sometimes disparagingly referred to as 'folk psychology' is actually the appropriate form of explanation for a vast range of human behaviour. The best way of understanding why people hold certain beliefs is usually to identify their reasons for holding those beliefs. The best way of understanding why people act as they do is to identify their reasons for their actions, the desires and values and emotions which motivate them. This is what explains, because it is what removes the particular puzzles by which we are perplexed.

The bogey of 'reductionism', then, is not a convincing threat to the humanist espousal of naturalism. The defence of naturalism is not a defence of reductionism, because there is no coherent reductionist programme to which it might lead. Naturalism does not threaten to lead to the conclusion that we are really 'just machines', or neural networks, or gene-machines, or computer programs. It is entirely compatible with the recognition of the great diversity and richness of human life and the diversity of explanatory frameworks by which we can come to understand it.

Dualism and the problem of interaction

If naturalism is so inclusive, is it vacuous? Does it actually exclude anything? Traditionally what naturalism has been seen to rule out is any belief in 'supernatural' entities. That label has increasingly come to be eschewed by critics of naturalism, who protest that they do not believe in 'spooky' beings such as disembodied 'spirits' or ghosts. Naturalism, however, is not just a rejection of the supernatural in that narrow sense. What it rejects is any talk of a separate 'domain of existence' or 'level of reality' distinct from the world which we know and inhabit. And its reason for doing so is that any 'two worlds' theory – any 'dualism' of this kind – will struggle to provide any coherent account of the relation or interaction between this world and the supposed 'other' world.

Two classic examples from the history of philosophy will illustrate this. The first is the idea that 'values' – things such as goodness, truth and beauty – have a special kind of existence, as 'timeless' realities, perhaps, set apart from this world. The second is the idea that the 'mind', or 'soul', or 'spirit', is something radically distinct from the components of the physical world. We will look at each of these ideas in turn, as a way of sharpening our understanding of what 'naturalism' means.

Plato, the famous Greek philosopher writing in the 4th century BCE, insisted on the objective existence of values such as goodness, justice and beauty. In what has come to be referred to as his 'Theory of Forms' or 'Theory of Ideas', he insisted that such values have a reality independent of whatever people happen to believe about them. These values can be known only by the mind, not by the senses, and are distinct from the existence of individual good people or individual just societies or individual beautiful objects. He made the same claim about mathematical entities. When mathematicians investigate the nature of 'the triangle' or 'the square' or numbers, they do so by the exercise of pure reason, not by sensory observation of individual squares or triangles or whatever. These perfect values and perfect mathematical objects, and perhaps other concepts too, Plato maintained, are pure eternal ideas, unchanging forms.[1]

Plato's problem was then how to provide a convincing account of the relation between these ideal forms and their particular instances – the relation between particular beautiful objects and beauty itself, or between particular triangles and the perfect form of a triangle. He attempted various formulations, such as that individual beautiful objects are 'copies' or 'images' of beauty itself, or that individual triangles 'participate in' the ideal form of the triangle, but it was unclear what these ways of putting it actually meant. Having emphasized so strongly the distinction between the ideal world known by pure thought and the physical world known by the senses, he was unable to bring them into any plausible relation with one another or to explain how the one could have any effect on the other. He had, as his pupil Aristotle scathingly put it, simply doubled the number of entities to be explained.

Our second classic example is the French philosopher René Descartes. Influenced by, and himself contributing to, the 17th-century scientific revolution and the mechanistic picture of the physical world that included human bodies and the bodies of other living things, he insisted that 'the mind' or 'soul' must be something distinct from physical things and from our own bodies. We can, whenever we think, be aware of our minds and their indubitable existence, even while we are ignorant of the workings of our bodies and perhaps even doubting their very existence. Therefore, he inferred, these must be two distinct kinds of existence. For Descartes, the 'two worlds' picture is a dualism of minds and bodies.[2]

Like Plato, he then had insuperable problems bringing his two worlds into relation with one another and explaining how minds and bodies can interact and affect one another. They must surely do so. We know, for instance, that when a sharp physical object pierces the skin it leads to the mental experience of feeling pain. We know that when we mentally form the intention of drinking a coffee, it normally leads to the physical action of raising the cup and drinking. But what can be the nature of the causal interaction here? We know how one physical event, by its physical impact, can cause another physical event – how one billiard ball, when it strikes another ball, can make it move. We know how one thought can generate other thoughts – how a memory of last year's holiday can evoke a nostalgic pleasure. But those two causal realms are each self-enclosed. Physical events, governed by causal laws which can be discovered by the physical sciences, can, it would seem, only cause other physical events. The world of the mind contains only our thoughts and feelings. Everyday experience suggests that the two kinds of entities must interact, but how can that be possible? Once the world of minds and the world of bodies have been separated, it is difficult to put them back together again.

Naturalism, of the kind presented here as the humanist framework of beliefs, rejects any such 'two worlds' picture, which will always have the insuperable problem of how to provide any positive account of the relation between the two realms of existence. And this naturalism has some radical implications.

'Mind' and 'spirit'

In spelling out those implications, perhaps the best place to begin is by picking up what Descartes said about the relation between minds and bodies. Naturalism, we have said, rejects Descartes's dualism of 'minds' and 'bodies' as two distinct kinds of entity, interacting but belonging in two different realms of existence. This does not mean that from a naturalistic standpoint we have to deny that human beings 'have minds'. Of course we have minds, in the sense that we engage in a vast range of activities which could be described as 'mental' or as having a mental dimension. We form intentions, we weigh up evidence, we hold beliefs and we debate them and argue for them, we feel angry or cheerful, we design gardens or pictures, we enjoy music, we read books. It could, in a colloquial sense, be said that in all such activities we use our minds. But problems arise if we focus on the noun 'mind' and if this then leads us to ask questions such as: What kind of thing is the mind, what is it made of? Is it a physical thing or does it consist of some other kind of substance? Where does it exist? Is my mind a part of my body or is it something different from my body, and could it continue to exist without my body?

As the philosopher Gilbert Ryle argued, in what is still the best discussion of 'the concept of mind', all these ways of talking involve what he called a 'category mistake'.[3] They go wrong by putting talk of 'the mind' in the wrong category, regarding it as though it were some kind of thing or entity, and then having to ask whether it is the same as or different from that thing which is 'the body'.

If we focus not on the noun 'mind' but, instead, on the language of verbs, adjectives and adverbs, we stand a better chance of avoiding the confusions so easily created by talk of 'mind' and 'body'. If we say that someone is engaged in the *activity* of 'painting a picture', this is, of course, a bodily activity, but it also carries the clear implication that she is 'using her mind', and it makes little sense to try to split off the 'mental' and the 'physical' components. Likewise, if we say that she is working 'carefully', that is a statement about her bodily behaviour, but the description of *how* she is doing it is equally an attribution of 'mental' features. If we describe her as 'skilful', we are attributing to her a certain kind of *ability*, an ability to perform what is in a sense a physical activity, but to do so in ways which exhibit what could also be called 'mental' abilities. Ryle's book *The Concept of Mind* is a comprehensive analysis of the innumerable linguistic resources with which we can talk about our mental states and actions without falling into the trap of supposing that there is some hidden internal arena, 'the mind', in which these activities take place.

Granted, not every individual mental activity is straightforwardly identifiable with a single piece of overt physical behaviour. It may not be obvious to others that I am silently humming a tune to myself, or enjoying the memory of last year's holiday, or wrestling with a difficult decision, but these are activities which I can engage in only as an embodied human being, only because I can also do these things out loud and communicate them to others, and because I have previously been taught by others how to do them and have learnt to copy their observable and audible behaviour. What Ryle refers to as the myth of 'the Ghost in the Machine' – the idea that these are the activities of a spectral non-physical entity which is the 'mind', contrasted with the equally specious idea of the 'body' as a purely mechanical object – is something which we are led to entertain only because we leave behind our everyday ways of talking and stray into misleading theorizing.

Naturalism, then, rejects the idea of 'the mind' as a disembodied entity, interacting with but distinct from 'the body'. And by the same token we should be equally sceptical of the third member of that modern holy trinity 'Mind Body Spirit', the classification frequently to be found in bookshops and catalogues. Humanists sometimes tend to be suspicious of the language of 'spirituality'. At one level, talk of something like 'spiritual fulfilment' is something to be embraced, and it is as central to humanism as it is to human experience. We can contrast the relatively superficial side of our lives with those activities which are 'spiritually' uplifting, such as listening to a magnificent piece of music, or an exhilarating walk over the hills, or the emotions of love and friendship. The problem with the word 'spirituality', however, is that it suggests something belonging to a special realm which is that of 'the spirit'. Describing someone as a 'spiritual' person can too easily imply that they are a devotee of esoteric 'spiritual practices' set apart from the texture of our everyday lives. In future chapters we shall need to find ways of talking about the importance of 'spiritual fulfilment' for humanism while avoiding those misleading connotations.

God

Here is a second radical implication of naturalism. With its critical stance towards talk of disembodied minds and spirits, it calls into question various religious ideas, not least traditional ways of understanding the concept of 'God'. Exchanges between atheists and those who believe in the existence of a deity, such as the God of the monotheistic religions of Judaism, Christianity or Islam, often take the form of debating the classic arguments for and against such a belief, and assessing the evidence. Theists may argue, for instance, that a belief in a divine creator is the best explanation for the order and appearance of design in the world. Atheists may counter that better explanations, more convincingly supported by evidence, are to be found in scientific hypotheses such as the cosmology of the 'big bang', or in evolutionary theory, which explains the variety of living species, and the process of natural selection, which explains why species are adapted to survive in their particular natural environment. These familiar arguments for and against the existence of a god have been batted to and fro for centuries. Taking a different approach, many religious believers will say that what counts for them is not so much these rational arguments but their personal experience of a God whose presence pervades their lives, guides and sustains them. But from the standpoint of naturalism we need to raise more fundamental questions about whether the very idea of a deity is a coherent one.

'God' is typically thought of as a non-physical being whose nature is defined by essentially mental attributes. God *loves* us, he sustains the world through his *purposes*, he *guides* us on the right path if we are willing to be guided, he *listens* to our prayers and *forgives* us when we fall short. It is, of course, open to theists to say that their God is in fact a physical being, like the gods of the ancient Greeks and Romans, who fought in their wars, and seduced those humans whom they found sexually attractive – aided though they were in these endeavours by their ability to render themselves invisible when necessary. But adherents of the monotheistic religions are likely to respond that this is an excessively anthropomorphic picture, and are more likely to say that, in the words of the Gospel of John, 'God is spirit, and those who worship him must worship in spirit and in truth'.[4]

The mental and spiritual concepts used to describe God's nature get their meaning, however, from our human interactions in the physical world. Love in all its many forms, for instance, is something whose meaning we come to understand from our physical interactions with one another, of caring and being cared for, of nurturing and sharing. It is not at all clear what it could mean to apply these concepts to a non-physical being. Even more problematic is the role ascribed to God of creating and sustaining the whole universe. God is supposed to be the ultimate explanation of why the physical universe exists, but the fact is that we simply have no idea how a non-physical being could generate physical reality. This is the problem of interaction writ large, the problem of making sense of the idea of another domain of existence standing in some intelligible relation to this world. Given the attributes and actions traditionally ascribed to God, then, it becomes difficult to see how any clear and coherent sense can be given to the understanding of 'God' as a spiritual rather than a physical being, a 'supernatural' being who nevertheless interacts with and intervenes in our world. It is at this fundamental level that naturalism undermines the traditional idea of a deity.

It is, of course, open to the religious believer to say that these are things we cannot understand, that we are talking the language of metaphor or mystery. More radically, thoughtful believers may reject this whole way of talking about God. They may say that God is not 'a being' at all, is not an individual entity added on to the rest of existence, and that to talk of 'God' is to talk not about 'a being' but about the nature of 'being' itself. They may say that the language of 'God' and religion is a way of talking about our deepest emotions, our sense of awe and reverence, our feelings of care and concern for the world and one another. We shall not follow that direction of thought here. It is not the business of this book to attempt a definitive 'refutation' of theism, or to suppose that there could be such as thing, bearing in mind the widely different forms which a religious stance can take. Humanists are likely to take varying attitudes towards these endeavours to reinterpret religious language, and some reinterpretations may be so radical as to be almost indistinguishable from humanism. But, from the humanist perspective, the preferred language will be the language of naturalism. If we want a frame of orientation with which to understand the world, we can stay with the rich language of shared human experience, with the language of creative writers, the poets and novelists, rooted in that experience, and with scientific explanations drawing on experience for evidence and confirmation.

One life

There is a further implication of naturalism which is perhaps more radical still. Since the idea of a free-floating disembodied 'mind' or 'spirit' can be given no clear sense, we have to embrace the fact that our lives end with our physical death. There is no immortal soul. And we know, from the scientific evidence, that all our mental activity is dependent on the functioning of the central nervous system and ceases when that ceases. In the search for some credible notion of immortality, the only other recourse would be to some idea of a transition to a new form of embodied physical existence – perhaps the belief in reincarnation to be found in some Eastern religions, or the belief in the resurrection of the body, which is one version of the Christian belief in life after death. Quite apart from the lack of evidence for such a post-mortem existence, however, there is the difficulty of explaining what this 'self' is which is imagined as transitioning from one body to another. In short, this life is the only life we have, just as this world is the only world there is – and those beliefs are at the heart of humanism.

For many people, and for most people at some time or other, the fact of human mortality can seem a heavy burden, a blow to our hopes. Most of us want to go on living. For the 20th-century Spanish philosopher Miguel de Unamuno, the fact that we must all die engenders what he called 'the tragic sense of life'. It is a deep human instinct to want our lives to continue, but reason can provide no convincing grounds for a belief in immortality, and it is this

Figure 2.1: White marble bust of Epicurus

The philosophy of Epicurus was a clear statement of the practical implications of naturalism, concisely summarized in what was referred to as 'The Fourfold Medicine': Nothing to fear in God. Nothing to feel in Death. Good can be attained. Evil can be endured. Lucretius's great verse presentation of this philosophy, *On the Nature of Things*, likewise counsels tranquillity in the face of death:

> What has this Bugbear Death to frighten Man,
> If Souls can die, as well as Bodies can?...
> For thou shalt sleep, and never wake again,
> And, quitting life, shalt quit thy living pain.
> But we, thy friends, shall all those sorrows find,
> Which in forgetful death thou leav'st behind;
> No time shall dry our tears, nor drive thee from our mind.
> The worst that can befall thee, measur'd right,
> Is a sound slumber, and a long good night.
>
> (Translated by John Dryden)

---

irreconcilable conflict between feeling and reason, he says, that is tragic. For Unamuno, the outcome has to be an irrational faith in the possibility of an eternal life united with the Universal Consciousness which is God. 'We must needs believe in that other life in order that we may live this life, and endure it, and give it meaning and finality.'[5]

The emotional need is not just for the continuation of our own lives. There is also the often intense longing to be reunited with those we have loved and have lost, a longing which can sometimes be unbearable. It may be so intense that we may be literally unable to believe that they are no longer alive. It is not surprising, then, that belief in some form of survival after death has been a prominent component of the major world religions, and that a significant number of people worldwide who are not religious or do not believe in a god nevertheless believe in a life after death.

Undeniably, death can be tragic. Losing a child who dies young is especially liable to be devastating. The unanticipated death of an adult in the prime of life, when they still have so much to give and so much to live for, is a cruel loss. The very idea of 'tragedy' as a dimension of human experience is closely tied to the fact of our mortality. But it does not follow that, because all our lives must end, the human condition is essentially tragic. Knowing that this life is the only life we have, and that we cannot live it again, may encourage us to live it more intensely, live it to the full, appreciating each moment. In the words of Matthew Arnold:

> Is it so small a thing
> To have enjoy'd the sun,
> To have lived light in the spring,
> To have loved, to have thought, to have done;
> To have advanced true friends, and beat down baffling foes;
> That we must feign a bliss
> Of doubtful future date,
> And while we dream on this
> Lose all our present state,
> And relegate to worlds yet distant our repose? ...[6]

We can say more. The fact that our lives could end at any time, and sooner or later will do so, is precisely what makes life precious. If life were eternal, then nothing would matter – not, at least, in the way that things matter in a finite life. The Swedish philosopher Martin Hägglund puts it well:

> Far from making my life meaningful, eternity would make it meaningless, since my actions would have no purpose. What I do and what I love can matter to me only because I understand myself as mortal. ... The question of what I ought to do with my life – a question that is at issue in everything I do – presupposes that I understand my life to be finite. ... If I believed that my life would last forever, I could never take my life to be at stake and I would never be seized by the need to do anything with my time.[7]

A frame of orientation

This, then, is the humanist 'frame of orientation'. Naturalism is a framework for our beliefs which builds on our day-to-day experience of the world and on the scientific hypotheses and theories which explain that world. It offers an overall perspective into which those beliefs most plausibly fit. It avoids the difficulties of a 'two worlds' view and the problem of how different realms of existence could interact and stand in some intelligible relation to one another. For naturalism, this world is the only world there is.

Not only is naturalism the framework of belief which makes best sense of the scientific approach, it is also the one which best enables us to make practical sense of our own lives. It grounds us in the familiar world of our shared experience and the texture of everyday life. It encourages us to recognize that these are enough. We do not need to posit another world, a heaven to come, or a timeless nirvana, to sustain our hopes. Julian Huxley, the first President of the British Humanist Association, identified the central idea of his humanism in words quoted from the Spanish-American philosopher George Santayana:

> There is only one world, the natural world, and only one truth about it; but this world has a spiritual life in it, which looks not to another world but to the beauty and perfection that this world suggests, approaches and misses.[8]

That is an appropriately modest use of the world 'spiritual', signifying that naturalism offers not a diminished view of our experience but a recognition of the manifold ways in which this world can inspire us. In the next chapter we shall look further at how we are able to find meaning in our lives through this embrace of the familiar. In its defence of naturalism, then, humanism offers a frame of orientation and devotion which makes theoretical sense and meets our practical needs. That is part of what humanism is for.

3
MEANING

Towards the end of the previous chapter, we began to raise questions about what makes a life *meaningful*. In doing so, we are broadening our enterprise to the search for a frame of orientation *and devotion* – that is to say, a framework not only for our theoretical beliefs about the nature of reality but also for our *practical* concerns, about how we should live and what we should live *for*.

Meaning and purpose

That reference to the idea of *purpose*, to the question of what we should be aiming for, sometimes leads critics of humanism to claim that it is incapable of providing an answer to the question of 'the meaning of life'. The assumption here is that there must be some pre-given plan or purpose which we have to discover; that this must be a plan laid out for us and for the universe as a whole by a divine creator who brought us into existence to fulfil that purpose; that it is revealed for us in the teachings of religion; and that humanism, in rejecting that way of thinking, is condemned to view life as meaningless.

This idea of an external purpose for human life, independent of our own aspirations, is also to be found outside the confines of conventional religion. The question 'What is the meaning of life?' is often rephrased as the question 'Why are we here?', with the implication that in order to have a meaningful life we must discover the purpose for which we have come into being. When something untoward happens to them, people often say, 'There must be a reason for it,' and they appear to mean that it must have happened for a purpose. It is an attitude expressed by the familiar phrase 'It was meant to be.' A significant number of people who say that they are not religious and do not believe in a personal god may say that they nevertheless believe in the existence of some 'higher power' or in 'underlying forces of good or evil' and appear to attribute to this impersonal power or force some kind of purposive agency.[1]

The charge against humanism that it makes life meaningless is also sometimes thought to follow from the fact of our mortality, as seen in the previous chapter. Unamuno, we saw, maintained that we must believe in an eternal life in order to give this life 'meaning and finality'. The novelist Leo Tolstoy famously wrestled with this thought. At a crisis in his life, he began to dwell on the inevitability of his eventual death and to feel that this made everything pointless:

> The truth was that life is meaningless. I had as it were lived, lived, and walked, walked, till I had come to a precipice and saw clearly that there was nothing ahead of me but destruction. ... My question – that which at the age of fifty brought me to the verge of suicide – was the simplest of questions. ... It was: 'What will come of what I am doing today or shall do tomorrow? What will come of my whole life?' ... It can also be expressed thus: 'Is there any meaning in my life that the inevitable death awaiting me does not destroy?'[2]

The line of thought appears to be that if what makes my life worth living is an orientation towards the future, a working towards future goals, and if that future is erased by my own death, then the edifice collapses.

Must life have a meaning?

From a humanist perspective, 'What is the meaning of life?' is likely to be seen as the wrong question – an inappropriate question. It implies that the challenge of giving a direction to one's life, of seeing one's life as worth living, can be met by discovering the right formula, by following the right script, one which is already written for us. And that way of thinking fails to do justice to the *personal* nature of the concern which may lie behind the question. If there is such a thing as a 'meaningful' life, then it has to be meaningful *for me*, something which gives *me* a reason for living and for trying to make the most of my life. Whatever the answer that may be offered – that the meaning of life is 'to worship and glorify God', or 'to help others', or 'to attain eternal life', or 'to pursue wealth and fame' – it will count as an answer only if it makes sense *to me*. If the offered answer leaves me cold, fails to inspire me or motivate me, then it is not an answer. Only I can give a meaning to my life.

Some would say that all talk of 'meaning' in this context is misplaced. We can ask for the meaning of a word or a sentence, but 'life', it might be said, is not the sort of thing which can have a meaning. That, however, is perhaps excessively restrictive. We do use the word 'meaning' more widely. A parent entering the house and finding a scene of mayhem may ask, 'What is the meaning of this?', and be told, 'We're playing hide and seek', and the answer may at least make sense of the chaos. Activities can have a meaning, so why not 'life'?

Questions about the meaning of life are ones which people do sometimes appear driven to ask, spontaneously, as an expression of dissatisfaction with the course of their life. It may not be one which regularly exercises people, carried along as they may be by the pattern of their daily life and its responsibilities. If they are in an extreme situation where all they can think about is how to make the pain stop or how to stay alive, asking 'What is life for?' becomes a superfluous luxury. If their existence is dominated by the struggle for survival, the question is unlikely to occur to them. Perhaps that is one reason why the language of 'the meaning of life' is primarily a modern phenomenon, characteristic of more affluent societies. But if one is in the relatively privileged position of being able to step back from life's immediately urgent demands and reflect on it, the question may arise. It may do so perhaps at a turning point in life – the breaking up of a relationship, the children leaving home, losing one's job or retiring from work – and being confronted with the prospect of loneliness or inactivity, or the need to rethink one's aims and aspirations. At the extreme, 'What's the point of anything?' is one way to articulate a certain kind of desperation.

Picking up the point about the need for the answer to be a personal one, however, some humanists would say that the mistake is to pose the question in general terms, as a question about the meaning of 'life', whereas one should be asking what makes *my* life meaningful. And that, they may say, is a matter for personal choice:

> the meaning of your life is the meaning you give it ...
> there is not one thing, a one-size-fits-all thing, that is
> 'the meaning of life'. People are various, life is various,
> circumstances differ; there are many ways that life can be
> good, flourishing and meaningful.[3]

On this view, the meaning of one's own life is something to be created rather than discovered.

There is an important truth there, but at the same time we should recognize that not just anything goes. There are limits to what could count as a meaningful human life. The life of a hamster in a cage, endlessly and repetitively trundling a wheel, could not be a meaningful life for a human being. We should remember also that for a great many people the character of their life is largely shaped by the nature of their daily work, and for some, the analogy of the hamster on a wheel may not be misplaced. A life in which the greater part of each day is spent, say, stacking shelves or operating a machine may well be one in which that person struggles to find meaning.

Recognizing, then, that people are various and that a huge variety of activities, goals and projects will give meaning and purpose to different people's lives, are there any general features which we can identify as necessary conditions for a meaningful human life? If so, how can a humanist perspective help us to do so?

Authenticity

We can begin from the point already emphasized, that a meaningful life has to have a *personal* significance. For my life to be meaningful, it must be *my* life. I must be able to recognize myself, my own traits and interests, in the way that I spend my life. We have seen that the humanist tradition has always placed a strong emphasis on the exercise of critical thought and independence of mind. Human beings are thinking beings. They cannot live simply on the basis of biological instincts. They cannot help forming their own beliefs, making their own choices and decisions. Humanism is characterized by the commitment to embrace that necessity, to recognize that we have to make our own judgements and decisions, to think for ourselves. But, as we have also noted, the social institutions within which we live our lives may make this difficult. The work which people have to do in order to survive may be structured and imposed by economic institutions which condemn them to lives of mindless drudgery, with no room for individual initiative. Oppressive political institutions and social conventions may make it dangerous for people to think for themselves. For some, the acceptance and internalizing of conventions may come easily, it may be no hardship to go with the crowd, but the humanist ideal of using to the full our distinctively human capacity to exercise our own thought and judgement may require a struggle. This is not to say that any meaningful life has to be iconoclastic, has to be startlingly original. But it has to be authentic. A meaningful life is not an alienated life, it cannot be one whose personal significance is stolen from me.

Creativity

Closely linked to personal authenticity is the importance, for a meaningful life, of creative activity – activity with which one makes one's mark on the world, gives expression to oneself and gives one's identity an objective existence. Artistic creativity is what immediately comes to mind, but that does not mean that to have a meaningful life one has to be a great artist. People play music, write poems and stories and reminiscences, paint and draw and make pots. And there are innumerable other activities which have a comparable significance – gardening, cooking, making clothes or patchwork quilts, decorating the house and making furniture. In these and many other ways, people make use of their own distinctive skills and give expression to them, and what they create says something about them. The popularity of such activities is familiar and unsurprising, and what it demonstrates is that in these seemingly mundane ways, without the need for any grand scheme of belief such as a religion, people can make meaning for themselves.

Karl Marx was one of the first thinkers to use the word 'humanism' in its modern sense, and it is in the context of his discussion of humanism, in his unpublished early writings, that he dwelt on the importance, for human beings, of their work on the world by which they not only produce to satisfy their material needs. 'It is in the working over of the objective world that man ... duplicates himself not only intellectually, in his mind, but also actively in reality and thus can look at his image in a world he has created.'[4] And this is true not only of the individual human being but also of our shared humanity; it is in the transformation of the natural world by our shared work and our distinctively human capacities that we become aware of our shared humanity imprinted on the world. The world becomes a human world, and, as Marx puts it, humanism and naturalism coincide.[5] A fundamental criticism of capitalist economic relations, for Marx at that stage in his thinking, was that the private ownership of the means of production and its products alienates human beings from their work and hence from their own humanity. Marx was writing at a time when, for many factory workers, the working day took up all their waking hours, leaving little or no room for creative activity in their leisure time which might provide scope for meaningful work and self-expression. For those of us in more fortunate and less oppressive circumstances, such creative activity can become an important aspect of our ability to find meaning in our lives.

Future generations and ongoing communities

Marx's emphasis on our shared humanity, and its reflection in a natural world transformed by human *social* agency, becomes very relevant if we return now to Tolstoy's agonizing about the apparent meaninglessness of his life. His crisis was triggered by confronting the fact of his mortality, and the thought that everything he lived for, his achievements and his purposes, would come to an end with his death. And the proper response to that fear is to remind ourselves that so much of what matters to us will *not* end when we die. This is true, above all, of our relations to other people, at every level. It is something we are aware of most vividly in our family relationships. We care about future generations – our children and grandchildren, or the children of others who are close to us. Our striving for their future, our wanting to leave the world in a better state for them, is one of the most important things which, for many of us, gives meaning to our lives.

The fact that future generations matter to us mirrors the way that past generations matter to us. Many people are fascinated by their family history. They feel that it helps them to define who they are. And even if we have no particular interest in tracing our ancestors, most of us are conscious of what we owe to our parents, and we see it as an important aspect of who we are. We are likely to feel grateful for what we have inherited from previous generations, or, if we are less fortunate, to see our lives as scarred by their legacy. Either way, most of us see ourselves as embedded in an on-going family history, so that what gives significance to our lives is shaped both by what we inherit from our predecessors and by what we bequeath to those who come after us. The meaning which we find in our lives, therefore, is not undermined by their finite nature. Mortality does not destroy meaning.

Recognizing the significance which family ties have for us leads to the wider recognition of how our lives are part of an on-going history at many levels. We belong to a local community. The past of the locality where we live may well have a particular fascination for us, giving us a closer attachment to the places we see every day, and by the same token we may be motivated to preserve that heritage, the buildings and trees and rivers which are part of our lives. Undoubtedly, also, a great many people take pride in their membership of a larger society, such as a nation and its history, and, at the extreme, that identity may lead to a willingness to die for their country. Such loyalties can, of course, become dangerously nationalistic, exploited by cynical politicians and promoting an exclusionary hostility to outsiders, but the feelings of allegiance are themselves real and often vivid. They are to be countered not by denying them but by recognizing the many other transnational commitments we have, to cultural and intellectual traditions, and their continuation into the future. And the fact is that a great many people care about the future of humanity as a whole. It matters to them whether we are wrecking our world for future generations or, on the contrary, cherishing it and trying to save it and enhance it.

At one level, all of this is obvious, but we need to be reminded of it because it counters the idea that we can find no meaning in a finite life. We do indeed need to see ourselves as part of something larger than our individual lives, something which was there before we were born and will continue beyond our deaths. This explains the appeal of looking for a purpose outside ourselves, such as a divine plan or providence, offered us as 'the meaning of life'. But that appeal can be resisted, and this is where the humanist reminder of the familiar comes into play. We can and do find meaning in the one life we have and the one world we inhabit.

The natural world

The sense of being a part of something larger than oneself is not confined to our relationships with past and future human generations. We can experience it too in our relation to the non-human natural world. Life flows on, the life of other species, and we are part of that continuing life. We are aware of the mysterious otherness of a kestrel on the wing, hovering and exercising its amazing powers of sight, or of the swallows which have arrived after a remarkable journey of thousands of miles, and at the same time aware of our kinship with them and with all living things – an awareness which has been enhanced by knowledge of the evolutionary process. Our investment in the future of non-human life is different from our care for future generations, but it is none the less real. Many people, for instance, including many humanists, take inspiration from the thought that after their death their body or their ashes will return to the ground and become part of the continuing cycle of the natural world – that in that very physical way they will continue. The 'something larger' also extends beyond living species. A proverbial case is the experience of looking up at the night sky, studded with countless stars and myriad other worlds, and experiencing what Sigmund Freud referred to as the 'oceanic feeling' – the sense of being dwarfed by the immensity of what we see, and at the same time being part of it. Once again these are familiar but vital experiences, ways in which we find meaning by transcending the limits of our finite human lives. And the awareness that the natural world is our home, to which we belong, is another aspect of the naturalism which humanism espouses.

The world of nature enriches our lives, of course, in ways which are not just captured by the idea of being part of something larger. We find meaning in our experience of the sheer beauty of nature – the view from the mountain top, the earth carpeted with spring flowers, the glow of autumn colours. 'Meaningful' is by no means the only epithet by which we might want to describe the value of such experiences, but they can make us feel glad to be alive, and if our time on earth in which to enjoy them is limited, that is all the more reason to relish them and take inspiration from them.

> Loveliest of trees, the cherry now
> Is hung with bloom along the bough,
> And stands about the woodland ride
> Wearing white for Eastertide.
> Now, of my threescore years and ten,
> Twenty will not come again,
> And take from seventy springs a score,
> It only leaves me fifty more.
> And since to look at things in bloom
> Fifty springs are little room,
> About the woodlands I will go
> To see the cherry hung with snow.
> A.E. Housman[6]

Meaning, mortality and stories

Returning, then, to the relation between mortality and meaning, let us recall Martin Hägglund's assertion, quoted in the previous chapter, that it is the very fact of one's mortality that is the condition for one's life being meaningful. 'Far from making my life meaningful,' he said, 'eternity would make it meaningless, since my actions would have no purpose. What I do and what I love can matter to me only because I understand myself as mortal.'[7]

MEANING

One way of elaborating this would be that my mortality gives a *shape* to my life. We can think of life as a *journey*, from birth, through the learning of childhood and youth, to mature independence, and then to old age and death. Particular events in a person's life will get their significance in part from their place in that journey. A youthful first love affair may be a step into the unknown; a new relationship later in life may be a second chance, or perhaps a problematic temptation. A first trip abroad may be an exciting exercise of independence; the same trip repeated many years later may be an occasion for nostalgic memories. Death itself, of course, has a very different significance at different ages: the death of a child is tragic, a heartbreaking loss to their family; the death of someone at the height of their powers is a different kind of tragedy, bringing a sense of terrible waste. The painless death in old age of someone who can look back over a life well lived may be sad, but it is not tragic.

This is not to say that everything will always fall into place. One may not necessarily view the course of one's life as a coherent unity. It may for a time be animated, for instance, by an overwhelming passion which is felt to be at odds with the general tenor of one's existence. But in due course, one is likely to feel the need to try to fit things together and ask what it all adds up to.

So, we can tell the story of a person's life, and of one's own life. Each story will be unique, made up of irreplaceable particular events and experiences, but each will be shaped by that generic narrative arc. We may or may not explicitly tell such a story about ourselves, as we look back on our lives, but most of us are likely at some time or other to think in those terms, to understand our ambitions and achievements, our hopes and disappointments, by placing them within an implicit life story. One person's life may be a journey through suffering and tribulation to the finding of happiness and serenity in old age. Another may be a story of youthful promise never fulfilled, leaving a wistful sense of what might have been. Or again, it may be a sequence of episodes, of career changes and radical new departures, going back into education, perhaps, or leaving a well-paid job in order to go travelling. Such stories may be told by others at a person's funeral, putting together the memories of family and friends and assembling them into a picture of who that person was. Certainly, it will be the centrepiece of a humanist funeral, and humanist funeral celebrants testify to the power of telling the story which gives meaning to the life that is celebrated at such a ceremony. That story can be told because it is the story of a finite life with a beginning, a middle and an end.

In telling such stories we are bound to be drawing on the repertoire of fictional stories which we have heard or read and which provide a template with which to understand the shape of a human life. Storytelling is a part of every human culture. As children we may be told fairy stories in which 'they all lived happily ever after'. We soon learn that life is not so simple. The reading or hearing of more sophisticated stories helps us, as we grow and learn, to make sense of the complexities, to fit them into a new and more nuanced

Figure 3.1: A humanist funeral

story of our own lives, to think about our experience as part of a story of the overcoming of adversity, or as a journey shared with others in evolving relationships.

To describe fictional stories as 'templates' does not mean deploying them as stereotypes, shoe-horning the particularity of our own individual experience into a hackneyed story. On the contrary, it is the limitless variety of fictional stories, of novels and films and plays, traditional and contemporary, popular and 'high art', that stimulates our awareness of the multiple perspectives from which our own lives can be read. Looking back on our experience, we may at first see it as fragmentary; we may then come to see how it can be shaped in different ways, how we can tell different stories about it, as success or failure, as coherent or contradictory. No one story is definitive; any story is only provisional, open to reinterpretation as one's life continues and falls into new patterns, and complete only with death. And it is perhaps with this idea of the 'story' of a life that the language of 'meaning' can most readily be seen to have its place. A story is the kind of thing which can be said to have a meaning, and just as we learn to interpret a fictional story, so we can find a meaning in our own experiences when we can tell a story about them and see them as hanging together or forming some kind of pattern.

The role of the aesthetic perspective can be extended more widely, beyond the shaping of events into a meaningful story. More generally, it is creative artists who can best enable us to recognize the manifold experiences in our lives which make them meaningful and worth living. It is the poet and the painter who capture the glint of the light on the water, the swans on the lake, the view from the hills, the glow of the setting sun, and who find meaning in our relation to the natural world. Likewise, it is the musicians and poets who can capture for us the feelings of love and loss, of triumph and despair, and remind us how they all have their place in a life seen as a meaningful whole. Even if we feel overcome with grief at the death of a loved one or the ending of a relationship, we can in time step back from the experience and recognize that this too is part of what it means to be human.

Humanism, I have said, following Erich Fromm, can be seen as a frame of *orientation* and *devotion*. There is the theoretical aspect – 'orientation', making sense of the world around us – and the practical aspect, making sense of what we live *for*. From the perspective of humanist naturalism, the need for a sense of purpose is to be met not by identifying some external purpose to which we must conform, but by identifying the purposes within our lives which make them worth living. Humanism does not offer a revelation of 'the meaning of life'; it reminds us of the familiar facts of experience, of the things which make our lives meaningful, and reminds us that they are enough.

Sometimes we may feel that they are not. Someone's life may fall apart. The ending of an intimate relationship, or the failure of a project to which their life has been devoted, may leave them feeling utterly bereft, that their life has become pointless. We know too that people may be cruelly weighed down by a state of depression which may seem unaccountable. But most of us can feel fortunate to be able to draw on those dimensions of experience which we have reviewed in this chapter, and which can give meaning to our lives. They are the facts of personal authenticity and creative activity; of our embeddedness in ongoing communities which link us to past and future generations and to things which matter to us beyond the limits of our finite lives; our relationships with the natural world and with other living things which likewise make us a part of something larger; and the shape given to our lives by the journey from birth to death, enabling us to tell meaningful stories about our own lives and the lives of other. These, for humanism, are the familiar facts which are the sources of meaning, and recognizing them is another aspect of what humanism is for.

4
VALUES

'Values are the new religion', according to Linda Woodhead in her Edward Cadbury Lectures with that title.[1] Talk of 'values' is, she says, ubiquitous and explicit. For younger generations they serve to define one's identity. Organizations such as schools and businesses adopt their own statements of values as a way of badging themselves. National identity too is increasingly defined in those terms; schools in the UK are required by law to promote 'fundamental British values', and 'Britishness' is defined by these values rather than as allegiance to King and Country.[2]

The shift is seen by Woodhead as both cause and effect of the decline of traditional religious institutions. The churches, she says, have lost their moral authority. The perception of them as hierarchical and censorious has combined with the loss of credibility resulting from moral scandals such as the perpetration of sexual abuse by the clergy and the failure to acknowledge or tackle it. When pressed on the question 'What is the meaning of life?', younger people are likely to answer it by articulating their values rather than invoking a religious or philosophical perspective.

Foundations

In view both of the declining influence of religious institutions in large parts of the world, and of the diversity of religious and non-religious beliefs which people can adopt, there is an obvious attraction in the idea of looking to values rather than beliefs as a shared basis for living together. We may believe in different gods or no gods at all, it may be said, but we can all recognize the values of kindness and compassion, fairness and respect. There is, however, a criticism to be addressed. Many religious people would say that even if, on the surface, the non-religious appear to share the same values, these can have no firm foundation if they are not grounded in religious belief. If values are simply a human creation, critics say, then they are fragile and variable, and different individuals and communities can come up with any purported values, however appalling. If some people think it right to make others their slaves, or to treat other races as inferior, or to massacre the innocent, or to practise child sacrifice, there is no way of showing, from a merely human standpoint, that they are wrong. The only way to be sure that our values, or anyone else's values, are the right values is to show that they are anchored in the will of a God who is the author and creator of the universe and whose authority can guide us on the right path.

An ad hoc response would be that the values of the various religious creeds do not appear to be any better grounded. At the practical level they exhibit just as much diversity. Note that all the examples just listed are forms of behaviour which have been endorsed by one religion or another at some time. But we need to go deeper than that ad hoc response. There are serious underlying questions here about how values can, if at all, be given a firm foundation, how they can be shown to be well grounded. This chapter will attempt a humanist answer to that question – a humanist account of values and their basis. Values can properly be given a *human* foundation, I shall argue, but that is as firm a foundation as we need. Values are grounded in our shared nature as human beings, and that is why they can be shared values.

Facts and values

To tackle this question, we again have to enter some rather difficult philosophical territory. Many philosophers have seen it as important to make a distinction between *facts* and *values*. Factual questions, it is said, are ones which can, at least in principle, be addressed by a combination of empirical evidence and rational argument, and that is the appropriate route by which to try to answer them. We can, at least sometimes, find out what is really the case, what the facts are, and the success of the sciences has demonstrated that this can be done. Values, it is said, are different. They are not attempts to say how things are, what the world is like. The place of values in our thinking is to guide our actions, to tell us *what to do*, not to tell us *what is the case*. What values we adopt will therefore be a reflection of our individual or collective desires and preferences. Values are simply what we choose to value, and different people may make different choices. If this distinction between facts and values is valid, then it may appear to open up humanism to the criticism that, if values are a human creation, there is no limit to what values humans may choose to adopt. The only way to ensure that our values are the right values, it may be concluded, is to base them not simply on our merely human choices but on the will of a divine lawgiver who has the wisdom and authority to guide our choices aright.

I want to look more closely at this distinction between facts and values. At one level, it is a plausible contrast. There is, of course, a difference between trying to establish what is the case and trying to decide how to act. However, the fact/value distinction is not, I want to suggest, an exclusive divide. Facts and values overlap. Some facts have values built into them, some facts have practical and moral implications. The relevant facts are facts about human nature, about human needs and human relationships. Along these lines we can develop a humanist account of values, based on those facts, and we can give values a firm foundation which can be recognized not just by humanists but by anyone. (What follows, it must be said, is not *the* humanist account of values, but one which I want to defend.)

Human needs

To show how such facts can provide a foundation for our values, a good place to start would be with the concept of human *needs*. There are facts about what human beings need, and those facts at the same time have implications for how we should act. We know how to establish, on good grounds, that someone needs something, and if that is established, it also counts as a good reason to try to obtain it.

Some needs are contingent and conditional. If you are travelling by train, you need a ticket. That is a factually true statement, and it is a good reason for getting a ticket – but only if you are travelling by train. There are other needs, however, which can be regarded as unconditional. There are what we can call 'basic needs', things needed by any human being just in virtue of being human. Human beings need food and drink, air to breathe, and shelter from the elements. These are survival needs – we cannot live without them. It is a plain fact that we need them, it is a fact about our biological nature as human beings, and it is a reason for any human being to want to obtain them. Granted, we can imagine circumstances in which someone might choose not to act on such reasons – an ascetic who wants to mortify the flesh in order to get to heaven, or a hunger striker, or a terminally ill person who wants to hasten their own death. But these are special cases, in which the reason any human being has for meeting such needs does not disappear but is outweighed by countervailing reasons specific to that person.

There is another class of needs which we might call 'functional needs'. Because of our nature as human beings, we all need the use of our limbs and organs in order to function. There is a continuum between these and survival needs. Without a functioning heart or functioning lungs, we cannot live, but beyond that, we need the use of our legs for mobility, the use of our hands and arms for manipulating things, the use of our senses for finding our way around in the world, our vocal organs for communicating, and so on. We can survive without these, but we can cope only if the loss of them is compensated for. The amputee may be able to manage with an artificial limb, the blind person may be able to find their way with a guide dog, a disabled person may manage with a human helper. But the reality of the needs is confirmed precisely by the fact that if they are not met, the lack has to be compensated for.

There are, then, established facts about the things we need in order to *survive* and the things we need in order to *function*. There are also things we need in order to *flourish*, and these are needs which take us further into the territory of values. I referred in Chapter 1 to the discussion of human needs by the American humanist and psychoanalyst Erich Fromm. As well as the need for a frame of orientation and devotion, he identified four other fundamental needs.[3] These too stem from our nature as creatures who cannot simply

Figure 4.1: Erich Fromm (1900–80)

Erich Fromm was born in Frankfurt am Main, Germany, in 1900, and trained and practised as a psychoanalyst, but left for the US in 1934 after the Nazis came to power. He continued his psychoanalytic work in the US and also held academic positions there and in Mexico. He published extensively. His first major book, which appeared in 1941 with the title *Escape from Freedom* in the US and *The Fear of Freedom* in the UK, was a psychological analysis of the roots of authoritarianism in Nazi Germany and social conformism in US culture. His development of a humanist ethics and politics in books such as *Man for Himself* (1947) and *The Sane Society* (1955) drew not only on his psychoanalytic experience but also on his work in social theory and on his Jewish heritage. He was recognized by the American Humanist Association as Humanist of the Year in 1966.

---

live by biological instincts but have to think and make decisions, employing our reason and imagination.

The need for relatedness: As human beings we are 'torn away from the primary union with nature', we are aware of our 'aloneness and separateness', our 'powerlessness and ignorance', and we need to 'find new ties' to take the place of biological instincts. This need, Fromm says, lies behind 'all passions which are called love in the broadest sense of the word'.[4]

The need for transcendence: We 'cannot be content with the passive role of the creature', we need to be a 'creator'. In the act of creation, a human being 'transcends himself as a creature, raises himself beyond the passivity and accidentalness of his existence into the realm of purposefulness and freedom'. In this need 'lies one of the roots for love, as well as for art, religion and material production'.[5]

The need for rootedness: We need the sense of being rooted in a place and a community. With the 'severance of his natural ties', a human being 'can dispense with the natural roots only insofar as he finds new human roots and only after he has found them can he feel at home again in this world'.[6]

The need for a sense of identity: A human being:

> may be defined as the animal that can say 'I,' that can be aware of himself as a separate entity. ... Because he ... has lost the original unity with nature, has to make decisions, is aware of himself and of his neighbor as different persons, he must be able to sense himself as the subject of his actions.[7]

There is nothing definitive about Fromm's classification of human needs. They could have been labelled differently, or counted differently. But it is a useful list. The second and fourth of these needs, it could be said, stem from our nature as distinct *individuals*, and the first and third reflect our nature as *social* beings. The importance of a balance between our individual identity and our collective identity is something to which I shall return in future chapters.

I have suggested that these are things we need in order to 'flourish', and it might be objected that this makes them only conditional needs. Different people, it might be said, have different ideas of how to flourish, some people value their independence and other people like being in groups, and so it just comes down in the end to personal preferences. However, it goes deeper than that. Notice that the basic needs identified by Fromm map neatly onto what we identified in the previous chapter as the things which typically give meaning to people's lives – personal authenticity, creative activity, community membership, and feeling part of something larger such as the natural world. As we acknowledged, people differ in the relative importance they attach to these things, but it is not just an arbitrary list which we can simply take or leave. So, the needs which Fromm describes can plausibly be seen as things which human beings need for a meaningful life.

As a psychoanalyst, Fromm describes the meeting of these needs as a condition of 'mental health', and that brings them closer to functional needs. They have to be met in order for us to function effectively. To recognize the force of the idea of 'flourishing' it is helpful to think of the distinctive ways in which human beings may fail to flourish. We may be lonely; we may be bored or frustrated; we may feel isolated and lost; we may feel crushed or oppressed. People vary in their resilience, and some can cope with such conditions better than others, but they are all debilitating, they are all impediments to full and effective functioning. That is why all human beings, however much they may vary, need some degree of independence and a sense of individual identity, and need some degree of support from others and a relationship to a social group of some kind. Think of the needs of other species. A dog needs to go for walks in order to flourish as a dog; a bird needs space in which to fly and cannot flourish in a cage, just as a tiger needs space in which to run and hunt. In similar ways the things which humans need in order to flourish go deeper than individual preferences. Whatever our specific individual idea of a good life, we cannot pursue it effectively unless these basic needs are satisfied, and meeting them is therefore a good thing for any human being.

Basic human needs, then, are firmly grounded values. From our knowledge of our human nature, we know that we need these things, and we know that this gives us good reason to act in certain ways in order to meet these needs. It is a knowledge which bridges the divide between facts and values.

Moral values and social relationships

However, at this point an obvious objection is bound to arise. These are not *moral* values. Even if it is granted that we can establish objectively what human beings need, and that this gives each of us good reasons to meet our own needs, it provides, it may be said, no reason why we should have any concern for *the needs of others*. What is distinctive of moral values, it is said, is that they are 'other-regarding', they are values enjoining us to show care and concern for other people, and it is impossible for any secular value-system to provide any secure basis for the value of altruistic concern. The underlying picture at work here is of humans as naturally selfish and incapable of responding to a morality which requires us sometimes to sacrifice our own interests for those of others. The gap can only be filled, it is said, by some external motivation such as guidance by divine wisdom or the prospect of otherworldly future bliss.

This picture should be rejected. Recall Fromm's list of basic needs. Human beings need other people. It is not just an instrumental need, a need for others to benefit us in various ways. We need positive relationships with others in order to flourish. We need the rootedness of belonging to groups or communities of some kind and being able to feel ourselves as part of them. Humans are social beings. We are all raised by at least one other person, we learn to live in the world by growing up with others, learning a shared language and with it a shared understanding of the world around us and shared patterns of behaviour.

A deep feature of our humanity, therefore, is the capacity for fellow-feeling – the propensity for sharing and being moved by other people's feelings of joy and sorrow, imagining how others feel and responding with *empathy*. It is something inseparable from our nature as social beings. Of course, that empathy may be all too limited, we may all too often sideline it or fail to act on it, and therein lies the problem, but the point to be established here is that, at however limited a level, such responsiveness to others is intrinsic to the human condition. Families and friendships, fraught though they may be, are a part of any human life. Within any family, however dysfunctional, there is at least the germ of care and concern. Ongoing sexual relationships, however abusive or exploitative, involve at least a minimal level of affection. A criminal gang will generate at least some feelings of loyalty and mutuality, however fragile and intermittent.

With those cautious ways of putting it, I have given full rein to pessimism. As a matter of fact, for vast swathes of the human population, things are nowhere near as desperate. Most people care for those they love. Many will at times make significant sacrifices for their children or their friends. They will sometimes cooperate wholeheartedly in shared tasks to which they are committed, in groups of which they feel a part. They will sometimes stand by their colleagues. They may even lay down their life for others or for their country, in however misguided a cause.

This is not a claim about the natural goodness of human beings. Humans also do terrible things, they all too often act with cruelty or with callous indifference. The claim to be made is that the capacity for at least some degree of empathetic concern is a deep fact about human beings, and it is a starting point, the place from which critical questions about the moral rights and wrongs of our behaviour can arise. What we can see as distinctively moral values are built into the social relationships in which we are all located.

The value of *honesty* is an inescapable norm inseparable from the use of language, from the activities of conversation and dialogue and the giving and sharing of information. Those activities would be

Figure 4.2: Margaret K. Knight (1903–83)

That moral values are independent of religious belief is now widely recognized, but the acceptance is not yet complete and it has been a slow process. An important step was the broadcasting by the BBC in 1955 of two radio talks by the humanist psychologist Margaret Knight with the title 'Morals Without Religion'. Much of what she said now comes across as simple common sense, but she encountered a great deal of opposition and procrastination from the BBC, and afterwards some vitriolic abuse from some of the press and the public, including newspaper headlines such as 'The Unholy Mrs Knight' and 'Godless Radio Repeat Shocks Nation'. The conclusion of her second talk remains highly pertinent:

> Why should I consider others? These ultimate moral questions, like all ultimate questions, can be desperately difficult to answer, as every philosophy student knows. Myself, I think the only possible answer to this question is the humanist one – because we are naturally social beings; we live in communities; and life in any community, from the family outwards, is much happier, and fuller, and richer if the members are friendly and co-operative than if they are hostile and resentful.

---

literally unintelligible without the recognition that their point is to convey what is the case. They are guided by the norm that, as the default presumption, we are telling the truth. The value of *fairness* is a norm built into the commitment to cooperation. It is not genuine cooperation unless it is a shared commitment, unless we are in it together and acknowledge the claims on us of our fellow cooperators that we do our share. The value of *loyalty* is inseparable from friendship. You are not a true friend if you are not prepared to stand by your friends. And underlying such values as honesty, fairness and loyalty are the fundamental values of *kindness, compassion and consideration*, rooted in the recognition of the other as a fellow human being. These are shared values, and they are shared because they are inseparable from the nature of human beings as social beings. Our living within a network of social relationships bridges the gap between facts and values.

To repeat: the inescapability of such values is no guarantee that we will act well. We may lose sight of them. We may misapply them. We may fail to recognize that a course of action may be unfair, or disloyal, or deeply dishonest. Or we may recognize it but succumb to other motivations. Notoriously, we are all human and we all fail frequently in just such ways. But as social beings we cannot escape the relevance of such values to our relationships with others and to how we regard them.

Why should I care?

And what if we fail? It is all very well, it may be said, maintaining that values are built into our social relationships, and that most people exhibit at least some degree of empathetic concern for others, but what if they don't? What if people just don't care – don't care about deceiving their friends, or letting down their colleagues, or caring for their children and family members? Does the humanist approach have anything to say then? Isn't this an insuperable problem for any attempt to base values on a purely human foundation?

Actually, it is a problem for *any* account of values. We are no better off if we locate values in divine authority. The question would still remain: what if people fail to act on those values? There are still no guarantees of goodness – as is evidenced by the litany of religious denunciations, throughout the centuries, of human weakness and frailty and indifference. What could, of course, be said from a religious standpoint but not from a humanist one is that if you fail to care, you will be punished after your death. But that is not an account of why people should care about values, it is simply telling them to care about something else, future rewards and punishments. And even that has a pretty limited track record.

So, the question 'Why do some people simply not care?' is indeed a deep problem, and there is no easy answer, but the answer has to be, I suggest, a humanist one in the sense that we have to look at the facts of human capacities and limitations. We have to ask why people are not more attentive to the needs and feelings of others, where being 'attentive' straddles the divide between cognitive awareness and emotional responsiveness. And the answer has to refer to the ways in which attentiveness is blocked by resentment and bitterness and self-pity, or is diverted by people's sometimes desperate preoccupations with their own physical or emotional survival. Becoming more attentive, being able to open ourselves up to the needs of others, partly depends on things outside our control, on the nature of the society in which we find ourselves, but it is also something which we can address by *paying attention*, by *thinking* about what others are experiencing, what it is like for them, and how we are responding.

Acting on our values also requires us to think about what they involve in particular circumstances. We have to draw on our experience to predict whether acting in certain ways will have consequences which will respect or violate those values. This is not always easy. If I withhold information from someone, will that mislead her, and would that be dishonest? If I tell someone that his behaviour is embarrassing, would that be an act of honesty or an unkind humiliation? The task of thinking about the consequences becomes all the more difficult if different values conflict. We have to use our reason to weigh them and assess them, and to do that we may need to use our insight to understand why they are important, and why some values may outweigh others.

And, of course, on a large scale there may be hugely difficult judgements to make. Would supporting a war be an act of loyalty which I owe to my country, or would it be a willingness to perpetuate a cycle of violence and suffering? Would building a solar park on a field be wanton environmental destruction or a necessary step to generate clean energy and reduce carbon emissions and thereby prevent avoidable suffering for future generations? Then there are, at a general level, the contentious social and moral issues which divide people – disagreements about abortion or assisted dying, about the treatment of refugees, or about how to balance the rights of transgender people against women's rights.

Moral disagreements and shared values

It is the intractability of these disagreements which leads some to say that without divine guidance we are left floundering and can do no more than fall back on our individual subjective preferences. But, in fact, these disputes arise in the way that they do because at a fundamental level we share core values, and disagree about the application of them. Consider the debates and disagreements about assisted dying, for example. A shared value in this debate is the value of *compassion*. Some would say that if a person – someone close to us – is terminally ill, in terrible pain and begging us to help them put an end to their suffering, then compassion should lead us to try to help them by hastening the agonizing process of dying. Others might say that if we really care for that person, we could never be responsible for ending their life. We have to think hard, then, about what 'compassion' means and what it requires of us in such a case. Another relevant shared value is that of respect for people's independence – what is referred to as respect for *autonomy*, people's right to make their own choices about their own lives. Some would say that this is what underpins the respect for life itself, but others would say that in a case like this, if a dying person has arrived at the decision that the only prospect life holds out for them is continued pointless suffering, and they long for it to end, then we should respect their wishes. So, again, the moral dilemma requires us to consider what respect for people's autonomy really means and what it requires of us.

The fact that we come to these tough moral dilemmas from a position of values which we share is what accounts for our sense of what is at stake, and why we are able to argue with one another and try to *get it right*. There are no shortcuts to answers, no simple rules or formulae. We have to make the best use of our reason and judgement, examine our values, assess the evidence and draw on our accumulated experience. But in doing this, we are working out how best to apply and act on the core human values which we recognize as good reasons for our actions.

The recognition of shared values as reasons for actions is not only built into our social relationships, but into the very activity of moral debate and dialogue. This is itself a social activity. It is discourse about how *we* should behave, what values *we* should hold and how *we* should apply them. In arguing with others and giving them reasons, we are recognizing one another as thinking and feeling beings like ourselves. We employ a shared moral language, a shared vocabulary, one which presupposes recognition of one another as beings with shared needs and shared concerns.

This, then, is what I see as a humanist approach to values. Once again it is rooted in the familiar – in the shared values which are part of our everyday lives and relationships, and which reflect the facts of our nature as human beings – facts about our human needs and facts about our relationships with one another. It is an approach building on the naturalism defended in Chapter 2. Starting from these core values, our ethical thinking can be extended to the difficult moral dilemmas and large-scale issues which beset us. Our sharing of a language of values is what makes rational debate possible.

Religious rules and core values

I have stressed that these core values are shared values deriving from our shared humanity, and that means, of course, that they are shared by those who are religious and those who are not. We do in fact find these core values recognized in the moral codes of all the world's religions, and that is important. But we also find, in some versions of those religions, moral rules of a different kind. People who belong to a particular religion sometimes insist that it is right or wrong to act in certain ways, not on the basis of any shared human values, but simply because the rules are enshrined in their own sacred scriptures and their institutional traditions. There are conflicts here between the humanist perspective and a certain kind of religious morality. This is an important qualification to what I have said about shared values, and something needs briefly to be said about it in conclusion.

The earlier discussion of basic human needs referred to the needs for relatedness and rootedness. For a great many people, one way in which that need is met is by a religious affiliation which is central to their identity. That need has to be respected. As we shall see in Chapter 6, it can be expressed in the language of *rights*, the basic human right to freedom of religion and belief. But an equally fundamental need, we saw, is the need for a sense of individual identity, the need for each individual to sense herself or himself as the subject of their own actions. This means that respect for people's right to belong to a religion must also encompass their right to reject a religion or to change their religion. This is common ground between humanists and a great many religious people, but there is also a long and continuing record of coercion and repression, forcing people to accept a particular religion and persecuting those who dissent. From a humanist perspective there can be no ethical justification for this.

Another important instance of the need for individual identity is the importance of people's freedom to express their authentic sexual identity. Again, we will look in Chapter 6 at the humanist insistence on the rights of gay and lesbian people. And again, many religious people will agree, but many will disagree, and historically the persecution of gay people has been a deep feature of certain religions which have typically served to perpetuate the traditional values of a particular culture. It is based not on any shared moral values but simply on particular passages in the sacred texts of the religion. It is that kind of religious morality, not humanism, that lacks any firm foundation.

One more classic example. Another basic human need, we saw, is the need for transcendence and creativity – the need to make the most of one's life, to develop one's own abilities and give creative expression to them. All human beings should be equally entitled to live their lives to the full, and it should go without saying that that means all women as well as men.

Notoriously, some religions have a long history of restricting the freedoms of women, denying them education or the freedom to work outside the home or to make their own choices and decisions. Again, as in the case of the condemnation of homosexuality, religious believers who accept these prohibitions appeal to scriptural texts as their justification, but those texts simply reflect particular cultural traditions rather than providing any objective moral basis.

It is, then, no surprise if, as Linda Woodhead observes, values are replacing traditional religion for a new generation. I have argued that this does not make values more fragile but, on the contrary, more secure, and humanism furnishes an account of why that is so. This, then, is a further answer to the question 'What is humanism for?'. As in previous chapters, a humanist account of values is rooted in the familiar and the everyday. It can show that values are grounded in facts about human nature, our human needs and our social relationships. These are shared human values and there is nothing original about them, but a humanist approach explains why these familiar values are important. It draws a contrast between them and one kind of religious morality. It recognizes why these values, though shared at a fundamental level, can give rise to deep moral disagreements. Once again what humanism offers is a framework, not a book of rules. We know how to think about what we ought to do. It is just that doing it in particular cases is sometimes demanding, and sometimes overwhelming, for our thinking and for our motivation. But that is not specifically a problem for humanists and for others who have no religious belief. It is a problem for everyone, religious or non-religious. It is the challenge posed by the complexity of human life.

5
COMMUNITY

What is *religion* for? A common answer is that organized religions provide for Believing, Behaving and Belonging. In previous chapters we have considered humanism as a non-religious framework for *beliefs*, and for the values which shape our *behaviour*. What about *belonging*? There is a case for seeing it as the most important of the three – that it is the 'belonging' that shapes people's believing and behaving. Defending the 'cultural paradigm' of religious transmission, Robin Gill has written:

> It starts from an eminently sociological presumption, namely that religious beliefs and values are shaped through religious socialization (formal or informal). Of course they may, in turn, shape religious practices and organizations, but they do need initially to be culturally embedded in human beings.[1]

Though people may sometimes come to be persuaded of the truth of a religious belief system and then, in consequence, join the appropriate church or other religious body, more commonly they inherit membership of the religious community from previous generations and imbibe its beliefs and values because they feel comfortable belonging in that community. In particular, for cultural or ethnic minorities, such as immigrant communities and their second-generation members, membership of the religious community can provide a strong sense of identity and the support which may be needed in a hostile environment. And, in a different context, it may happen that people join a church because they are looking for a community where they can feel at home, and going along with the set of beliefs is a matter of vague acceptance rather than careful scrutiny.

Belonging, churches and the Ethical Societies

Does the historical decline in religious affiliation leave a significant gap? Does it erode the opportunities for belonging? There are, of course, innumerable other kinds of community to which people belong – families, groups of friends, neighbourhoods, sports clubs and other interest groups, political parties and so on. I referred in the previous chapter to Fromm's account of the need to belong, and because it is such a fundamental human need, it is inescapably met at some level, even if inadequately. Everyone belongs to some kind of human community. The question, however, is whether there is something irreplaceable in the nature of religious communities and the needs which they meet.

Some have thought so. In particular, it is suggested that membership of a religious community furnishes the indispensable motivation for ethical behaviour. Without that support, the commitment to charitable giving or to altruistic self-sacrifice will be, it is said, difficult to sustain. In previous chapters, humanism has been presented as a frame of orientation and devotion. But if it is not rooted in a strong community held together by the explicit affirmation of shared beliefs and values in the manner of a church or other religious group, is humanism built on shifting sands? We are returning here, from a different direction, to questions raised in the previous chapter. Maybe values do not need the backing of divine authority, but do they need the support and structure provided by a religious community?

Some of the early non-believers in the 19th century felt that, in rejecting the Christian Church, they needed to replace it with some kind of secular church. The extreme example was the French positivist philosopher Auguste Comte, who devised a 'religion of humanity' for a Positivist Church with its own elaborate system of rituals and priesthood. His *Positivist Catechism* (1851) ordained the practice of private prayer for two hours every day, in three sessions: when rising, in the middle of the day, and in bed at night. Prayers were to be addressed to the figure of Woman as Mother, Wife and Daughter, guardian angels representing the past, present and future. Public worship was to take the form of 84 celebrations spread through the year. There were to be seven sacraments marking the stages of life from birth, through education, marriage and the choice of a profession, to death. John Stuart Mill, who had his own very different understanding of a 'religion of humanity', commented on 'the extraordinary height to which he carries the mania for regulation. ... It is this which throws an irresistible air of ridicule over the whole subject ... there are passages in his writings which, it really seems to us, could have been written by no man who had ever laughed.'[2]

Comte's excesses were fully deserving of Mill's scathing comment, but as the beliefs of the Christian churches came increasingly to be seen as unacceptable, the idea grew that the role of the churches should be taken up by new active communities dedicated to strengthening people's commitment to ethical values. This gave rise to what came to be known as the 'ethical movement'. As we saw in Chapter 1, Felix Adler, a young scholar from a Jewish background, established in 1876 the New York Society for Ethical Culture, to give lectures and sermons on ethical matters and to engage also in charitable projects and social reform such as the provision of healthcare. Other ethical societies were founded in Chicago, Philadelphia and St Louis, and the movement spread to Britain, with the setting up of the London Ethical Society (at first called simply the Ethical Society) in 1886. Its aim was 'to organise systematic Ethical Instruction in connection with such educational agencies as the Society for the Extension of University Teaching, Working Men's

Figure 5.1: Conway Hall, in Red Lion Square, London

Conway Hall preserves a historical link with the early Ethical Societies. It was opened in 1929 as the new home for the South Place Ethical Society, which had previously met in Finsbury, and was named after Moncure Conway, a former leader of the society. It continues to host talks, lectures and concerts, and is a popular venue for humanist events. It houses the Humanist Library and Archives. A virtual tour of Conway Hall is available at https://understanding humanism.org.uk/conway-hall-virtual-tour/

Colleges, Clubs, Co-operative Societies, and with the education of the young'.[3]

A large number of other Ethical Societies were set up across the UK in the last decade of the 19th century and the first third of the 20th, organizing an impressive range of activities including lectures not only on morality and ethics but also on scientific, social, political, intellectual and cultural topics, as well as debates, social meetings and soirées, leisure activities (music, dancing, tennis, rowing, cycling and nature rambles), and tea parties for poor children. The emphasis was on secular activities as the basis of ethical communities, but included also the singing of hymns, and the movement had its own hymn books. The West London Ethical Society went furthest in replicating the practices of the Christian churches. It held Sunday services in its own church building in Bayswater from 1909, and in 1914 the Society renamed itself the Ethical Church. In the vestibule of the building were portraits of famous humanists including Thomas More, John Milton, Matthew Arnold, Lord Tennyson, Joseph Mazzini, Robert Browning, Elizabeth Barrett Browning and John Ruskin. The interior contained decoration by the Arts and Crafts artist Walter Crane, busts of the goddess Athene and of Socrates and Marcus Aurelius, statues of Jesus and of the Buddha, and stained-glass windows depicting Joan of Arc flanked by Elizabeth Fry and Florence Nightingale. The order of service might include an organ voluntary and an introit, a canticle, an intoned Statement of Belief, anthems and hymns.[4]

The Ethical Church was led by the charismatic American Stanton Coit. It was something of an outlier, and the character of most of the ethical societies was more strongly secular. The Union of Ethical Societies was established by the UK societies in 1896. Renamed in 1920 the Ethical Union, it became in due course the British Humanist Association, now Humanists UK. The movement and its local groups have continued to organize meetings, talks and social events, but the use of hymns and sermons has long been discarded. The tradition of holding Sunday meetings retaining something of the character of church services but without the traditional Christian creeds and rituals has been continued in the UK by the Unitarians and

COMMUNITY

in the US by the Unitarian Universalists, both of which movements draw on the humanist tradition as well as on Christianity and other world religions.

Humanist organizations at local, national and international level do provide communities of support for humanists, and in many parts of the world, where humanists face persecution and in some cases risk their lives, that support can be vital. In the UK, besides the existence of local groups enabling fellow humanists to meet and talk, Humanists UK runs a programme called 'Faith to Faithless', which provides peer support for people leaving high-control religions, and has sections such as 'LGBT Humanists' providing a community for particular groups of humanists. Trained celebrants provide humanist ceremonies – funerals, weddings and naming ceremonies – for the non-religious, who may well not be members of any humanist organisation but who want to mark these rites of passage in a way which is consonant with their beliefs.

Humanist weddings provide a ceremony in which couples can celebrate their commitment to share their lives within a context of a shared world view. Humanist funerals enable people to share their grief, to share their memories and to celebrate a life, recognizing that we have only one life and that each person lives it in their own unique way about which a unique story can be told. All these activities can be properly described as the provision of humanist communities, but they do not fully replicate the role which the Christian churches traditionally filled in the wider community. That, it has to be said, is not what humanism is for. So, the

Figure 5.2: A humanist wedding

question remains: with the decline of the churches, does this leave a gap?

Social capital

An affirmative answer might seem to be suggested by two influential pieces of sociological work over the past half-century, focused particularly on the US. Robert Bellah and his colleagues, in *Habits of the Heart*, published in 1985, drew attention to the corrosive effect on American public life of the culture and language of individualism.[5] The churches had historically been an important countervailing influence drawing citizens into public life. 'Religion', the authors wrote, 'is one of the most important of the many ways in which Americans "get involved" in the life of their community and society.'⁶ Despite the separation of Church and State, the various Christian denominations had functioned as an established church at the local and state level, with church leaders serving as a moral authority enjoining their members to perform their civic duties. But with the diversification of the US population, religion itself became more private and diverse. By the 1850s, 'in place of the colonial township unified religiously and politically around a natural elite, religion operated with a new emphasis on the individual and the voluntary association'.[7] Nevertheless, the churches, through these voluntary associations and societies, continued to draw their fellow citizens into wider concerns such as the issues of temperance and slavery. More recently, differences had emerged between the liberal and conservative churches in the degree to which they encouraged a reaching out to engage with the needs of the wider community, but the churches had continued to furnish a community of personal support for their members, 'a loving community in which individuals can experience the joy of belonging'.[8]

Fifteen years later, in the book *Bowling Alone*, Robert Putnam identified what he saw as a more recent stage in the decline of community involvement in the US.[9] He made use of the concept of 'social capital', defined as 'the connections among individuals' social networks and the norms of reciprocity and trustworthiness that arise from them'.[10] The concept implies that participation in face-to-face community groups such as churches has benefits for the wider society. Putnam argued that social capital in the US grew in the period after World War Two until the 1970s and then went into decline as people's lives became more privatized. His claim applied not only to churches – his title refers to the decline in bowling clubs – but he maintained that 'Faith communities in which people worship together are arguably the single most important repository of social capital in America'.[11] He quoted figures to indicate that church members were substantially more likely to give to charity and volunteer for charitable and philanthropic activity. The decline in religious participation from the 1970s onward was therefore to be seen as an important dimension of the growth in individualism and the decline of social capital.

Putnam made an important distinction between two dimensions of social capital, which he referred to as *bonding* and *bridging*. Communities are good at bonding if they create strong in-group loyalties which provide social support for their members and give them a strong sense of belonging. They are good at bridging if they promote values of altruistic and humanitarian service which is not just directed at serving fellow members of the group but also extended outwards to the wider community. The concept of 'social capital' relies on the idea that bonding also encourages bridging but, as Putnam acknowledged, it does not necessarily do so. There is, as he says, a 'dark side of social capital'. 'Social capital is often most easily created *in opposition* to something or someone else.'[12] In other words, the easiest way to cement the bonds of group membership is to stir up fear of a common enemy against whom everyone has to be united. We can call this 'bonding by exclusion'. I want to suggest that it is this phenomenon, and the ambivalence of the relation between bonding and bridging, that must be kept in mind when we think about the historical and continuing role of churches and other religious communities in societies such as the US, Britain and other European countries where their numbers are falling.

Bonding and bridging

Religious communities, because they are built around commitment to a structure of beliefs and values, do have a special potential to promote in their members a willingness to look beyond their own interests and preoccupations to the needs of others. However, they also, by their very nature, have a propensity to foster bonding by exclusion. A group of people held together by shared beliefs and values, not just by the fact that they live together or enjoy spending time together, is especially liable to identify itself by the contrast with groups defined by different beliefs and values.

There have been and are, of course, a great many religious people inspired by their beliefs to do wonderful work to better the lot of their fellow human beings, to look beyond their own religious community and try to make the world a better place. Impressive examples are the role of Christians such as Martin Luther King in the civil rights movement, working with other Christian denominations and secular political groups to combat racial segregation and discrimination; the role of liberation theology in championing the cause of the oppressed, especially in Latin America; and the continuing work that churches and other religious organizations do to combat poverty, support refugees and so on. These are examples of both 'bonding' and 'bridging', drawing on the strength and cohesion of a religious community to reach out to those in need.

At the same time, looking around the world today, we see all too many cases of governments and demagogues mobilizing religious allegiances to bolster nationalistic and political enmity and hatred – the appeal of extreme right-wing populism to the evangelical churches in the US, the role of Catholicism in Eastern Europe and the Orthodox Church in Russia, Hindu nationalism in India, the bitter conflict between Judaism and Islam in the Middle East, the persecution of Rohingya Muslims in Buddhist Myanmar. And the bonding which nurtures these inward-looking exclusive loyalties is typically generated not only at the national level but by local communities, and gives rise to hatred and violence at that level.

Meeting the need for belonging

In a modern diverse and pluralistic society, there is a great variety of groups and communities which meet the need for belonging. Sports clubs, exercise classes, book or film groups, art clubs, choirs, meditation sessions, education classes, workplace networks and friendships – the list can easily be extended. In the past, churches have been good at meeting the need, but in a society such as modern Britain, especially in an urban context, there are innumerable other places where people can find connection and support. Not everyone manages it, some people are lonely, and the loneliness of the big city can be especially painful, but neither religious communities nor any other kind of social grouping can be guaranteed to provide the belonging which people need. What is distinctive of religious communities, I have acknowledged, is that they are built around a shared frame of orientation and devotion. They encourage their members to think about their beliefs and values and to act on them. That, however, as I have also emphasized, can have both its benefits and its dangers. What is most important, from a humanist perspective, is that people should not be confined to a community which simply reinforces their own beliefs, but that they should encounter other beliefs held by other groups. Bridges can be crossed in both directions. If social capital is to promote bridging, it has not just to provide the opportunity to reach out to others in order to help and serve them, but also to listen to them and learn from them.

'Think for yourself' is a sound humanist slogan, central to the humanist tradition. Religious communities are not always good at encouraging people to think for themselves. They may do so, but in practice they often promote conformity and orthodoxy. What stimulates people to think for themselves is above all the encounter with those who think differently. We need criticism, argument, disagreement. A humanist view of community will therefore value not only support and belonging, but also the diversity of overlapping communities which is characteristic of modern societies and encourages engagement with difference.

What remain to be seen are the ways in which and the extent to which new forms of community and belonging are being created by digital technology. According to a recent study, members of Gen Z born around the turn of the millennium, who have grown up with the internet, are finding new ways to use online communication to establish 'fine-grained identities' which affirm their individual authenticity, and at the same time to search out a subtle variety of communities which reflect the different facets of their identity. These are new and supportive 'communities of values', which mean that individuals are no longer, as they might once have been, trapped within the closed communities into which they are born but with which they do not identify.

> Contrary to a stereotype that views every recent generation as more individualistic than the prior one, postmillennials are finding and forging new modes of community that lessen the contradictions between being a *me* and being a *we*. Far from 'bowling alone' or 'Generation Me' gazing narcissistically into their screens, many young people are as concerned about belonging as they are about finding who they really are, and they do not necessarily see the two as distinct.[13]

On the other hand there is the ubiquity of algorithms bombarding online users with content which matches their stereotypes, reinforces their prejudices and fosters echo chambers. The danger is that of creating narrow communities which are all too tightly geared to new kinds of bonding and exclude bridging.

Humanism, then, does not itself seek to replace religious communities with new kinds of communities. It does generate a view of the value of community, and of the particular kinds of communities which are important in meeting human needs. It enables us to welcome the diversity of overlapping communities which is characteristic of modern societies. It celebrates the need to think for yourself along with the need to belong, to bond but also to bridge, to listen to, talk to and engage with others who think differently.

6
POLITICS

It is an open question whether there is a distinctive humanist politics. For reasons to be explained, humanism does not neatly align with what would be conventionally labelled either a left-wing or a right-wing position. Nevertheless, humanist values do have political implications. One of the defining features of humanism, we have seen, is the commitment to free and independent critical enquiry. This is the starting point for the relationship between humanism and politics, and the best way to illuminate that relationship is to look at its history.

Rights: Thomas Paine

We have seen that modern humanism draws inspiration especially from the ferment of thought represented by the 18th-century Enlightenment. That espousal of free thinking and a willingness to reject traditional beliefs and institutions found political expression in the French Revolution and in the 1789 'Declaration of the Rights of Man and of the Citizen'. The Declaration is built around the value of individual liberty. Article 1 asserts that 'Men are born and remain free and equal in rights ...', and in Article 4 liberty is defined as 'being able to do anything that does not harm others'. This leads in Article 6 to the principle that all citizens, being free and equal, should have the right to participate in political life and choose their own representatives.

A vitally important right, reflecting the Enlightenment defence of free critical enquiry, is the right to freedom of religion or belief and freedom of speech and expression. Article 10 declares: 'No one may be disturbed on account of his opinions, even religious ones, as long as the manifestation of such opinions does not interfere with the established law and order.' This is reinforced in Article 11, which asserts that 'The free communication of ideas and of opinions is one of the most precious rights of man.'

These commitments to human rights, to free thought and free expression and to democratic government are unquestionably at the heart of any humanist approach to politics.

In Britain the advocacy of these rights and freedoms was undertaken most famously by Thomas Paine, whose deist stance was mentioned in Chapter 1 as an important contribution to the humanist tradition. Paine's humanism is exemplified in his book *The Age of Reason*, in which he sets out what he describes as his 'individual profession of faith':

> I believe in one God, and no more; and I hope for happiness beyond this life.
>
> I believe in the equality of man, and I believe that religious duties consist in doing justice, loving mercy, and endeavoring to make our fellow-creatures happy.
>
> But lest it should be supposed that I believe many other things in addition to these, I shall, in the progress of this work, declare the things I do not believe and my reasons for not believing them.
>
> I do not believe in the creed professed by the Jewish church, by the Roman church, by the Greek church, by the Turkish church, by the Protestant church, nor by any church that I know of. My own mind is my own church.
>
> All national institutions of churches – whether Jewish, Christian, or Turkish – appear to me no other than human inventions set up to terrify and enslave mankind and monopolize power and profit.[1]

As a deist, Paine maintains that the only clear meaning which can be given to the word 'God' is that of the 'first cause' of all things, whose effects are apparent in the order and magnificence of nature.[2] He contrasts a faith based on the contemplation of nature with a faith based on supposed 'revelation', and he proceeds to pour scorn on the Jewish scriptures – 'a history of the grossest vices, and a collection of the most paltry and contemptible tales'[3] – and on the New Testament accounts of the Virgin Birth, the bodily Resurrection of Jesus, and the performance of miracles. These are to be distinguished from the historical figure of Jesus, 'a virtuous and amiable man' who 'preached most excellent morality, and the equality of man'.[4] Paine's positive creed, then, was a faith in reason, in the equality of mankind based on the shared possession of reason, and in using one's own reason to form one's own beliefs. In the language of his day, he described this not as 'humanism' but as 'the pure and simple profession of Deism'.[5] We can see how this creed was for Paine a foundation for the defence of the French Revolution, of political equality and human rights, which he had set out a few years previously in *The Rights of Man*.

The First Part of *The Rights of Man* was published in 1791 and the Second Part in 1792. It was an instant bestseller, its radical ideas were hugely influential and it led to a government campaign against him and a charge of seditious libel. He was found guilty in his absence after he fled to France, only to be arrested by the French authorities after opposing the execution of the King, and he eventually escaped to America, where he died.

Paine's assertion of human equality is couched in characteristically deist language, drawing on the vague idea of an original creation but not tying it to any one traditional religious authority.

> Every history of the creation, and every traditionary account, whether from the lettered or unlettered world, however they may vary in their opinion or belief of certain particulars, all agree in establishing one point, *the unity of man*; by which I mean, that men are all of *one degree*, and consequently that all men are born equal, and with equal natural right ...[6]

Figures 6.1 and 6.2: Thomas Paine and Mary Wollstonecraft

Thomas Paine and Mary Wollstonecraft were late 18th-century radicals who combined free-thinking about traditional religion with the struggle for equal rights and representative democracy. Both of them were imperilled by their independent radicalism. Both travelled to France in 1792 to see at first hand and support the Revolution, but both of them were supporters of the Girondin faction and their lives were at risk when the Girondins were overthrown by the Jacobins. Paine was imprisoned and narrowly escaped execution. To add to Wollstonecraft's plight, she had an affair with an American businessman, Gilbert Imlay, and gave birth to a daughter, Fanny. She eventually managed to return to England, was abandoned by Imlay, and then met and married the radical philosopher William Godwin and had a second daughter, but died from the complications of childbirth. Her daughter by Godwin, also called Mary, continued the tradition of free thought and free love by eloping with the poet Shelley, whom she eventually married and by whom she had a child. Mary Shelley is most famous as the author of the novel *Frankenstein*.

This leads him to reject any form of government based either on religious authority (such as the idea of the Divine Right of Kings) or on military force and conquest. He attacks also the idea of inherited authority and an inherited right to rule, which robs every subsequent generation of its right to make its own reasoned choice of government. Commenting on the idea that an individual or a class might inherit the abilities needed to govern well, he says that 'an hereditary governor is as inconsistent as an hereditary author'.[7] The system of government which he recommends, in contrast, is that which he refers to not as 'democracy' – a term which he reserves for the direct democracy of some of the ancient Greek city-states – but as *representative* government, what is now referred to as 'representative democracy'.

Sexual equality: Mary Wollstonecraft

The belief in human unity and equality was put to radical use also by Mary Wollstonecraft, who moved in the same circles as Paine and courted the same dangers. As I have emphasized, the term 'humanist' in its modern sense was not then in use, but its applicability to Wollstonecraft, despite her occasional use of theistic language in her writing, is attested by her husband William Godwin in his memoir published shortly after her early death:

> Her religion was, in reality, little allied to any system of forms; and, as she has often told me, was founded rather in taste, than in the niceties of polemical discussion. Her mind constitutionally attached itself to the sublime and the amiable. She found an inexpressible delight in the beauties of nature, and in the splendid reveries of the imagination. But nature itself, she thought, would be no better than a vast blank, if the mind of the observer did not supply it with an animating soul. When she walked amidst the wonders of nature, she was accustomed to converse with her God.[8]

That primacy given to the contemplation of nature rather than the creeds of organized religions is an obvious similarity with Paine. Like him, she founds her political stance on the belief that what makes us human is the possession of reason, and that this is the basis of political equality. In defending the idea of equal human rights, she had anticipated Paine with the publication of her *Vindication of the Rights of Men* in 1790, and followed it with the groundbreaking *A Vindication of the Rights of Woman* in 1792. Asserting the natural equality of all human beings, male and female, she asks:

> In what does man's pre-eminence over the brute creation consist? The answer is as clear as that a half is less than the whole; in Reason.[9]

Reason, she says, is

> the power of discerning truth. Every individual is in this respect a world in itself. More or less may be conspicuous in one being than other; but the nature of reason must be the same in all ...[10]

If it appears otherwise, if women give the appearance of being creatures of emotion rather than reason, it is because they are confined to a social role in which their principal aim is to please and attract men, and are educated with that end in view.

> Pleasure is the business of a woman's life, according to the present modification of society, and while it continues

> to be so, little can be expected from such weak beings. Inheriting, in a lineal descent from the first fair defect in nature, the sovereignty of beauty, they have, to maintain their power, resigned their natural rights, which the exercise of reason might have procured them, and chosen rather to be short-lived queens than labour to attain the sober pleasures that arise from equality.[11]

The foremost right which she champions for women is, accordingly, an equal right to education.

Democracy and freedom of the press: Richard Carlile

A representative figure in early 19th-century Britain, continuing the legacy of Paine and Wollstonecraft, was the publisher Richard Carlile. He explicitly followed in Paine's footsteps, both in his humanism and in his politics. He published Paine's works including *The Rights of Man* and *The Age of Reason*, which he sold divided into short sections in order to make them easily affordable. This was a time of increasing agitation for parliamentary reform and extension of the franchise. Carlile was due to be one of the speakers at the demonstration in St Peter's Fields in Manchester in 1819 calling for political reform and the relief of poverty, but the meeting was brought to an abrupt and bloody end by the military who cut their way through the crowd, killing 18 people and seriously injuring many hundreds in what became known as the Peterloo Massacre. In the periodical *The*

Republican, which he edited and published, Carlile excoriated the Prince Regent for having, through the Home Secretary, Lord Sidmouth, congratulated the magistrates and the Yeomanry for 'their prompt, decisive, and efficient measures, for the preservation of the public tranquillity'. Carlile's letter to the Prince Regent ended with the bold warning:

> whilst the extreme of luxury and dissipation is enjoyed by one portion of the community, at the expence and destruction of the necessaries of life for the other – whilst the laws are violated, and murders are committed in open day, by those in whose hands the sword of Justice has been placed – and whilst the violation of those laws, and those murders committed, receive the sanction of the constituted authorities, I think I may safely affirm, that we have arrived to that stage of society, when every liberal and constitutional writer has argued the necessity and the justice of a People appealing to their *dernier resort*, an appeal to force, to annihilate the existing order of things, and to begin *de novo*. Reflect on this, Sir, ere it be too late.[12]

Carlile was charged with blasphemous libel (for publishing *The Age of Reason*) and seditious libel – charges reflecting his challenge to both the established church and the political authorities – and was imprisoned. He continued to write and publish from prison, in particular upholding the importance of free speech and freedom of the press. In his *Address to Men of Science* in 1821, he called on scientists to uphold the value of scientific education:

POLITICS

Figure 6.3: The Peterloo Massacre, engraving by Richard Carlile

This engraving of the 1819 Peterloo Massacre was published by the freethinker Richard Carlile with the following dedication:

> To Henry Hunt, Esq., as chairman of the meeting assembled in St. Peter's Field, Manchester, sixteenth day of August, 1819, and to the female Reformers of Manchester and the adjacent towns who were exposed to and suffered from the wanton and fiendish attack made on them by that brutal armed force, the Manchester and Cheshire Yeomanry Cavalry, this plate is dedicated by their fellow labourer, Richard Carlile.

Carlile exemplifies the links between radical politics and the radical criticism of traditional religious belief in the early 19th century.

Then come forward, ye Men of Science, it is reserved for you to give the death blow, or the last blow to superstition and idolatry. ... The many unnatural distinctions which Kingcraft and Priestcraft have brought into society, have totally undermined the first object of the social state. In addition to this universal evil, those two crafts have set themselves up as a bar to all useful improvement. ... The

> printing press has come like a true Messiah to emancipate the great family of mankind from this double yoke.[13]

Another of Carlile's publications, in 1828, was *Every Woman's Book*, the first book in English to give advice on contraception, which shocked the devout by suggesting that women as well as men should be able to enjoy sexual pleasure. This commitment to upholding women's reproductive rights has been another of the freedoms long championed by the humanist movement against ecclesiastical opposition. In 1877 Annie Besant and Charles Bradlaugh, leading members of the National Secular Society, were brought to trial for republishing the birth control booklet by the American Charles Knowlton, *The Fruits of Philosophy*. They were found guilty but released on a legal technicality.

On liberty: John Stuart Mill

These themes – the defence of basic human rights and freedoms including freedom of speech and expression; sexual equality and women's rights including access to education and reproductive rights; and democratic representative government – were given a thorough rational foundation in the work of the great 19th-century humanist philosopher John Stuart Mill. I mentioned in the previous chapter his scathing criticism of Auguste Comte. Mill himself embraced the idea of the 'Religion of Humanity', but his version was very different from Comte's. He understood by it the cultivation of 'the sense of unity with mankind, and a deep feeling for the general good'.[14]

Such sentiments, developed by education, can, he argued in his essay *The Utility of Religion*, provide a firmer and better basis for social morality and individual conduct than supernatural religion. The title of that work alerts us to Mill's belief that the test of the value of actions and institutions is their utility, but, he stresses, 'it must be utility in the largest sense, grounded on the permanent interests of man as a progressive being'.[15] Full human happiness is achieved only through the development and exercise of 'the qualities which are the distinctive endowment of a human being', the 'human faculties of perception, judgement, discriminative feeling, mental activity, and ... moral preference'.[16] This ideal of the full development of our distinctively human potentialities informed his elaboration of a humanist politics.

In his essay *On Liberty* of 1859, Mill argues for liberty of thought and discussion on the grounds that the free and open exchange of views is essential in the search for truth. It is needed for three reasons. The first is that, if our existing beliefs are false, we will not come to see this unless we listen to criticism of them. Secondly, even if our existing beliefs are true, it is only by having to answer those who disagree with us that we can fully understand why they are true. And in the third place, it is often the case that the full picture we need to arrive at is a combination of some of the beliefs which we hold and some of the beliefs which others hold.

Likewise, freedom of action is to be defended and promoted because 'the free development of individuality is one of the leading essentials of well-being'. Again it is a matter of the full development of our distinctively human capacities.

> He who lets the world, or his own portion of it, choose his plan of life for him, has no need of any other faculty than the ape-like one of imitation. He who chooses his plan for himself, employs all his faculties. He must use observation to see, reasoning and judgment to foresee, activity to gather materials for decision, discrimination to decide, and when he has decided, firmness and self-control to hold to his deliberate decision.[17]

Note that he sees the impediments to the free exercise of individuality as coming not just from the law and political power but also from the tyranny of custom and convention. Invoking the same criterion as we found in the French *Declaration of the Rights of Man and of the Citizen*, he maintains that the only reason for which either public opinion or legal restraints should restrict people's freedom is to prevent harm to others.

The promotion of people's exercise of their faculties is also an important part of Mill's case for democratic institutions. His *Considerations on Representative Government* was published in 1861, prior to the 1867 Reform Act, when the franchise was still extremely limited and excluded most working people. His defence of representative government appealed

Figure 6.4: John Stuart Mill, steel engraving, 1866

John Stuart Mill was a towering figure in British philosophical, political and economic thought in the 19th century. He made compelling cases for freedom of thought and expression, for sexual equality, for representative government, and for the freedom of individuals to live their own life in their own way provided they respect the same freedoms for others. Mill always insisted that the ultimate foundation for moral and political beliefs was the utilitarian principle of *the greatest happiness* as the ultimate end of human actions. But he also emphasized that what constitutes happiness or pleasure for a human being depends upon the exercise of our distinctively human capacities, and that the most fully human pleasures are 'the pleasures of the intellect, of the feelings and imagination'. In a famous passage he declares: 'It is better to be a human being dissatisfied than a pig satisfied; better to be Socrates dissatisfied than a fool satisfied.'

not just to the fact that people needed to have the vote in order to protect their interests. Even more important, he said, is the stimulus to the active side of the human character:

> The maximum of the invigorating effect of freedom upon the character is only obtained when the person acted on either is, or is looking forward to becoming, a citizen as fully privileged as any other.[18]

Mill was himself a Member of Parliament from 1865 to 1868, and in the debate on the Reform Bill he proposed an amendment to the legislation, changing the word 'man' to 'person'. This was the first time that anyone in the House of Commons had argued for extending the vote to women as well as men.

Mill's commitment to sexual equality, like so much else of his thought, was enriched and strengthened by his relationship with Harriet Taylor, his companion and collaborator, who in due course became his wife. Her own essay *The Enfranchisement of Women* was published in 1851. Mill's *The Subjection of Women*, drafted after his wife's death in 1858 and published in 1869, is his comprehensive case for full equality between men and women in marriage, in the world of work and culture, and in political life, and his answer to all the prejudices and objections with which it has to contend. The foundations of that case for women to play a full part in the life of society are, he says, not only the social benefits 'consisting in an increase of the general fund of thinking and acting power', but also:

> the most direct benefit of all, the unspeakable gain in private happiness to the liberated half of the species; the difference to them between a life of subjection to the will of others, and a life of rational freedom. After the primary necessities of food and raiment, freedom is the first and strongest want of human nature.[19]

With this vision of a full human life, making the most of one's abilities and developing one's faculties, Mill provides an appropriate humanist underpinning for the commitments to human rights, freedom of speech and action, democratic politics and social equality.

These political commitments, then, have been historically linked to the humanist tradition, in Britain and elsewhere. They have manifested themselves in the struggles for racial equality, for instance, and for gay rights. All these political values which were once marginalized and embattled have, at least in Britain and many other countries, become mainstream. I am not suggesting that the struggle for them has been exclusively humanist, but humanists have been at the forefront. It continues today, and in some parts of the world it is a desperate struggle against oppression. It is enshrined in the principles of Humanists International, as formulated most recently in the Amsterdam Declaration of 2022:

- We affirm the worth and dignity of the individual and the right of every human to the greatest possible freedom and fullest possible development compatible with the rights of others. To these ends we support peace, democracy, the rule of law, and universal legal human rights.
- We reject all forms of racism and prejudice and the injustices that arise from them. We seek instead to promote the flourishing and fellowship of humanity in all its diversity and individuality.[20]

How much equality?

I have said that humanist politics is underpinned by the idea of human equality. This idea now needs to be considered a little more closely. The underlying conception is what we can refer to as *moral equality* – that all human beings have the same moral standing and should all be treated with equal consideration and respect. It is a short step from this to *political equality* – that all the members of a society should have equal democratic rights such as the right to vote and to express their political views. More contentious is the idea of *economic equality*, and this is where legitimate disagreements might open up within a humanist perspective. The early radicals such as Paine, Wollstonecraft and Carlile certainly saw their challenging of political authority as going hand in hand with the struggle to combat poverty and the inequality between rich and poor. With the emergence of socialist and working-class organizations in the latter part of the 19th century, there was considerable overlap between the membership of these and of secularist and ethical societies. Annie Besant, whose championing of women's reproductive rights we noted earlier, was also a pioneer of the trade union movement, famous for her organizing of the match girls' strike in 1889. Talks and lectures at meetings of the Ethical Societies often included contributions from prominent socialist thinkers.

New questions for humanist allegiances were raised by the Bolshevik Revolution in Russia in 1917. Where many on the European Left were willing to give it their support, the humanist philosopher Bertrand Russell was one of the first to recognize, well before the atrocities of Stalinism, that Russian Communism was a new form of authoritarianism. After a visit to Russia in 1920, he welcomed the attempt at 'a fundamental economic reconstruction', but rejected the methods being adopted to achieve it:

> Bolshevism is not merely a political doctrine; it is also a religion, with elaborate dogmas and inspired scriptures. When Lenin wishes to prove some proposition, he does so, if possible, by quoting texts from Marx and Engels. A full-fledged Communist is not merely a man who believes that land and capital should be held in common, and their produce distributed as nearly equally as possible. He is a man who entertains a number of elaborate and dogmatic beliefs. ... This habit, of militant certainty about objectively doubtful matters, is one from which, since the Renaissance, the world has been gradually emerging, into that temper of constructive and fruitful scepticism which constitutes the scientific outlook. I believe the scientific outlook to be immeasurably important to the human race. If a more just economic system were only attainable by closing men's minds against free inquiry, and plunging them back into the intellectual prison of the middle ages, I should consider the price too high.[21]

In the period of the Cold War, Erich Fromm was at the forefront of attempts to articulate a 'Socialist Humanism' which could challenge the dehumanizing social structures of both Western capitalism and Soviet Communism. In this project he drew on the newly discovered early writings of Karl Marx and his discussion of work and alienation. Fromm assumed that a capitalist economy could deliver material affluence and that the task of socialist humanism was to transform the nature of work to make it the expression of human productive potential and creativity.[22]

This leaves unsolved the problem of economic inequality, which, despite Fromm's sanguine expectations, has greatly increased throughout the modern world. Some would argue, however, that any attempt to eliminate such inequalities would require unacceptable restrictions on individual liberty. In any society where people are free to use their abilities with the aim of bettering themselves, it is argued, some will be more successful than others and inequalities will always re-emerge. Hence, it is said, a would-be egalitarian society will turn out to be an authoritarian one, and the politics of redistributive justice will be incompatible with the liberal democratic values which we have seen to be linked to humanism.[23]

The counter-argument is that inequality erodes democracy. Unequal wealth brings with it unequal power. The beneficiaries of economic inequality are not just enterprising individuals but vast corporations and the people who run them. Their decisions can determine the priorities and direction of national economies; they have greatly disproportionate access to communications media and are able to influence the flow of information; they fund political parties and can effectively lobby politicians to get what they want. Insofar as individual liberty means people's freedom to make their own choices about the sorts of lives they want to lead, those choices are greatly constrained by the power of the wealthy.

There are contested empirical questions here, and the different answers which are given typify what are labelled as the political Right and the political Left. Humanism does not dictate answers to those questions, and they are matters on which humanists can reasonably disagree.[24] Hence my statement at the beginning of this chapter that humanism does not align neatly with one or another of the conventional political stances.

Environmental politics

There is one other element of humanist politics which it is important to mention. The political values which we have considered so far have all involved human rights and human interests. Humanism is sometimes criticized on the grounds that the word implies a concern only for human beings. That is a misunderstanding. Humanism is 'human-centred' in the sense that it emphasizes human responsibility and the fact that there is no superhuman power on which we can rely. But this is inseparable from the recognition that human beings are part of the natural world and have a responsibility to care for it. An active concern for the natural environment and for other living things is therefore an essential part of humanist politics.

This includes working to end practices such as factory farming which inflict unnecessary suffering on non-human animals. It means campaigning to protect biodiversity and ecosystems, and against threats such as the destruction of forests and the pollution of land

and water from agricultural and industrial activity. It means giving humanist support to the urgent action needed to combat global heating and climate change. Human interests are at stake here, of course, and in particular the recognition of our responsibility to future generations. But what drives environmental politics above all is the understanding that human well-being and the well-being of other living things are inseparable.

A key humanist figure here is Julian Huxley, the first President of the British Humanist Association. He was instrumental in championing the word 'humanism', but his preferred full label for the position he advocated was 'evolutionary humanism'. As a distinguished biologist he played a major role in formulating and popularizing the modern evolutionary synthesis bringing the Darwinian theory of natural selection together with modern genetics. A controversial and disturbing aspect of Huxley's work in genetics was his interest in and support for eugenics, something which he shared with many of his intellectual contemporaries.[25] More positively, however, he made a vital contribution to the linking of humanism and environmentalism. He was one of the first to emphasize the need for environmental action to focus not just on individual living things and species but on ecosystems, and this informed his own work for nature conservation. In his role as the director-general of UNESCO, he helped to set up in 1948 the International Union for the Protection of Nature, later renamed the International Union for Conservation of Nature and Natural Resources. He was actively involved in the establishing of wildlife reserves in Africa. He exemplifies the humanist application of scientific knowledge to ethical and political values.[26]

Humanist politics as I have presented it in this chapter is, in keeping with previous chapters, the politics of the familiar. In much of the modern world, the political values of human rights and basic freedoms, of democracy and of environmental protection, are in theory uncontroversial. Lip service is paid to them even if practical action lags way behind. But though these values are familiar, they are by no means secure. They cannot be taken for granted. They are relatively new in human history. In those countries where they are now accepted, they were in the quite recent past revolutionary. They had to be fought for. Humanists were part of that fight, often, as we have seen, running the risk of imprisonment or death. Across the world today these political values are under threat, and they have to be defended. In many countries, questioning the dominant religion, or criticizing the government, comes at great personal cost. In many countries, women and gay people are oppressed and crushed. Viewed in that light, humanist politics is highly controversial.

7
CONCLUSION

The question 'What is humanism for?' was, in Chapter 1, located in the context of the decline in religious affiliation in many (though not all) parts of the modern world. In subsequent chapters we have seen that humanism is not a replacement for religion, but that it does address some of the needs traditionally met by organized religions. It is what, following Erich Fromm, I called a 'frame of orientation and devotion', a broad way of thinking about the nature of the world and our place in it. Humanism, as we have seen, is a form of naturalism – the view that this world is the one world there is, and that human beings are part of the natural world. There is no non-natural realm separate from this one, and no non-physical form of existence which we will experience after we die. Humanism does not tell people how to live their lives, but it does point to the ways in which we can give meaning to our lives on the strength of our experience and our relationships to other human beings and to the rest of the natural world. It provides a firm basis for the core values which we live by, grounding them in our nature as human beings, our human needs and social relationships. It applies those values also to political life, and historically humanists have been at the forefront of struggles for human rights and human equality, democratic institutions and the protection of the natural environment. The articulation and defence of these beliefs and values is what humanism is for.

That is the humanism presented in previous chapters. This concluding chapter will look briefly at some criticisms of humanism, before returning to the question of why it is needed.

Is humanism just another religion?

The first criticism to be considered is the accusation that humanism is itself just another religion, sharing important features of the creeds which it claims to have jettisoned.

Some humanists have embraced the word 'religion' and repurposed it. John Stuart Mill, we saw, advocated what he referred to as a 'Religion of Humanity'. Julian Huxley called his evolutionary humanism 'Religion Without Revelation'. They were using the word in a way importantly different from its traditional sense. Humanism is not a creed, not a set of doctrines to which people are expected to subscribe. It does not appeal to any non-human authority for its beliefs and values. It draws on a rich tradition of thought and writing but it does not have any sacred texts. It promotes reasoned debate about the application of ethical values, but it does not insist on a set of detailed moral rules. It values supportive communities, and ceremonies in which people can come together to mark important staging-posts in their lives such as the welcoming of a new baby, the celebration of a marriage or the death of a loved one, but it does not promote communities of worship built around prescribed rituals.

Critics of humanism have sometimes called it a 'religion' and used the word is a disparaging sense. Yuval Noah Harari has written: 'The humanist religion worships humanity, and expects humanity to play the part that God played in Christianity and Islam ...'.[1] That description is a caricature which bears no relation to anything that any actual humanist has ever maintained. Humanists recognize that human beings are natural organisms, the products of an evolutionary process. As such, we humans are deeply imperfect, inheriting a complex mix of instincts and characteristics which may conflict with one another and damage our aspirations for our own lives and our relationships with one another.

Harari says that humanists treat human feelings as an infallible touchstone by which to settle questions in morality, politics, aesthetics, economics and education. The fact is that humanists and all human beings often get things wrong, we are often led astray by our feelings, and that the only recourse we have is to look critically at our mistakes and use reasoned thought and argument to try to get things right. Humanists do not worship humanity.

CONCLUSION

A naive faith in progress?

A different slant on the same accusation has been provided by the writer John Gray. He says:

> For its followers the religion of humanity seems different from the religions of the past. Having repudiated monotheism, they imagine that they stand outside the view of the world that monotheism expressed. But while they have rejected monotheist beliefs, they have not shaken off a monotheistic way of thinking. The belief that humans are gradually improving is the central article of faith of modern humanism.[2]

Gray's description of humanism as a 'faith in progress' is based largely on selective references to John Stuart Mill and Bertrand Russell. His attribution to humanists of a monotheistic belief rests on the assertion that 'A story of redemption through divine providence was replaced by one of progress through the collective efforts of humanity'.[3] On this he comments:

> The belief that humanity makes history in order to realize its full possibilities is a relic of mysticism. Unless you believe the species to be an instrument of some higher power, 'humanity' cannot do *anything*. What actually exists is a host of human beings with common needs and abilities but differing goals and values.[4]

No humanist would disagree. Humanism does not involve any belief in 'humanity' as an autonomous collective agent guiding the activities of individuals and guaranteeing social progress. Humanists, like others, may talk of having 'faith in humanity' as an expression of hope and resilience, but it is a 'faith' grounded in day-to-day experience of the potential of individual human beings to inspire and be inspired.

In attributing to Mill a faith in progress, Gray quotes Mill's reference to 'man as a progressive being' which was mentioned in Chapter 6. But as we saw, Mill is there talking not about social progress but about individuals as beings with potentialities for flourishing which they can develop if they are given the freedom and the means to do so. In a passage in his essay *Utilitarianism*, Mill affirms his belief that individual human beings are in themselves capable of living happy and fulfilled lives, but recognizes that the main impediments to this, the 'great sources of physical and mental suffering', are external factors such as poverty and disease. This is where human happiness depends on the prospects for social progress and improvement.

> The main stress of the problem lies, therefore, in the contest with these calamities, from which it is a rare good fortune entirely to escape; which, as things now are, cannot be obviated, and often cannot be in any material degree mitigated. Yet no one whose opinion deserves a moment's consideration can doubt that most of the great positive evils of the world are in themselves removable, and will, if human affairs continue to improve, be in the end reduced within narrow limits.[6]

He went on to say that although attempts to remove the causes of poverty and disease are 'grievously slow' and will be the work of many generations, the

CONCLUSION

Figure 7.1: Bertrand Russell

Bertrand Russell, the most famous British philosopher of the 20th century, was a committed humanist and a supporter of the British Humanist Association. In 1927 he gave a talk in London for the National Secular Society, 'Why I am not a Christian', which ends with his view of progress as something which is possible, but only if human beings employ 'a fearless outlook and a free intelligence'. In his later years he became a household name as a campaigner for nuclear disarmament, acutely conscious that the possibility of nuclear war was a threat to all hopes for human progress. His BBC broadcast in 1954, 'Man's Peril', ended with these words:

There lies before us, if we choose, continual progress in happiness, knowledge, and wisdom. Shall we, instead, choose death, because we cannot forget our quarrels? I appeal, as a human being to human beings: remember your humanity, and forget the rest. If you can do so, the way lies open to a new Paradise; if you cannot, nothing lies before you but universal death.[5]

---

struggle is in itself rewarding. Mill was writing in Victorian Britain at a time when a belief in progress was commonplace. In that context Mill's position can be seen as one of cautious optimism. It is at odds with the relentless pessimism which pervades Gray's own writing elsewhere, but it is not a naive optimism.

A century and a half later, we are more conscious (as was Bertrand Russell) of the terrible things which human beings can do to one another. We know that the human species might completely destroy itself, by nuclear war or by environmental destruction. Humanists will differ in their degree of confidence in human progress. All that is intrinsic to humanism is the belief that the betterment of the human condition is *possible* if human beings make the right use of their powers of reason and compassion.

Posthumanism and transhumanism

A further criticism levelled against humanism, which sometimes goes hand in hand with the criticism that it is just another religion, is the claim that it has had its day and has, in its turn, been superseded. The labels 'posthumanism' and 'transhumanism' have been used to indicate what will replace it.[7] The terms are used in a variety of ways but one idea which has been popular in some quarters is that of using the techniques of biotechnology and computer programming to transcend human limitations, in particular the limitations built into our biology. There are predictions of being able to overcome the physical processes of ageing and perhaps even death, maybe by uploading the contents of one's brain to a computer programme using inorganic hardware. There is the idea of making increasing use of artificial intelligence (AI) for decision-making superior to anything we can achieve with our limited biological brains. At the extreme are science-fiction scenarios of cyborgs (artificially enhanced humans) or androids (constructed of entirely non-human technology and AI) supplanting human beings.

CONCLUSION

Such ideas tend in the direction of fantasy, and it is not clear that even the more realistic versions of them are coherent. In particular, they appear to rest on the assumption that the human activities which are to be replaced, surpassed and transcended by AI can all be reduced to information processing. But the more modest versions of these attempts to overcome ageing and death, even if feasible, raise serious questions about the desirability of such aspirations. Of course, there are innumerable specific regrets and frustrations which come with growing old, and we may understandably wish that we could still do the things which we were able to manage 20 years ago. Of course, if our lives are still rewarding, we want them to continue and we try to ward off the prospect of their coming to an end. But at a deeper level, these things are integral to the ways in which we give meaning to our lives – and here the considerations discussed in Chapter 3 come into play. Our plans and projects make sense only against the background of a finite human life and the unfolding stages of that life. A timeless condition would be one in which we would lack reasons for aiming at one thing rather than another. Thinking through the idea of overcoming our human limitations may properly lead us back to a humanist perspective as the standpoint from which to consider whether it would be truly desirable.

In the meantime, existing developments in AI pose very real and urgent challenges. They are used to deceive and to spread misinformation, for example by creating text or recordings falsely attributed to someone, by doctoring photos and videos and by straightforwardly disseminating falsehoods. They are used to incite violence and hatred and to make it easy to send abusive messages. They promote inclinations to self-harm on the part of vulnerable people, including the young. All this is exacerbated by the use of algorithms which ensure that users of social media are targeted with more of the same rather than anything which challenges their behaviour and assumptions. Vast amounts of information can be gathered about people's behaviour, giving some people great power to manipulate others. And in these ways, oppressive political regimes can crush opposition.

This is not technology in control, taking over from humans. It is the consequence of human decisions, taken to promote the political interests of demagogues and dictators, and the economic interests of powerful individuals and corporations. It can be countered only by other human actions. And these actions have to be informed and inspired by the values which we have seen to be at the heart of humanism – the values of independent thought and critical enquiry, of reasoned debate between a diversity of views, of democratic engagement and holding power to account, and of human equality. These are values which are widely shared including by broadly humanist strands in the world religions, and it is vital that they are acted on by all who share them.

Digital technology has great potential to further those values. It can be used to access information with unprecedented ease, and to promote debate. It can bring

CONCLUSION

people together to challenge power and to organize opposition to oppressive regimes. It can facilitate greater democratic participation. Although these values are widely shared, in many parts of the world they are under attack, by authoritarian nationalism and other repressive ideologies. That is why it is all the more important to understand how important they are, how they have their firm foundation in human nature and human needs, and it is why humanism is needed now more than ever.

From the mundane to the inspiring

The theme running through previous chapters has been that humanism is rooted in the familiar and the everyday. The core moral values identified and defended in Chapter 4 are not unique to humanism. In many contemporary societies they are, or should be, familiar common ground, although there may be sometimes deep disagreement about their practical implications. The political commitments discussed in Chapter 6, commitments to critical enquiry and free speech, human rights and democracy should be uncontroversial, at least for most of the likely readers of this book. Likewise, the naturalistic worldview explored in Chapter 2 starts out from our everyday experience of the world, our dealings with the things around us, with our fellow human beings and with other living things. Humanism, then, is not an esoteric new doctrine, not a startling revelation of some great new truth. In an important sense it is a reminder and a reassertion of what we already know. To some this may seem disappointing, but it need not be so.

Humanism affirms what is 'mundane' in the literal sense of being 'of this world', but it does not follow that it is 'mundane' in the sense of being uninspiring. This world has all that is needed to inspire us. Although the everyday world is the one world there is, our everyday experience is not all there is to know about it. The ordinary can also be seen to be extraordinary.

The natural sciences, building on our everyday sense-experience, have dramatically extended our knowledge of the world. Over time they have shown that the universe we inhabit is truly remarkable. They have revolutionized our understanding of its extent in space and time. The universe does not revolve round our little plot of earth on our planet. Our sun is one of billions of stars in one of billions of galaxies, and the shift in our understanding of our significance in cosmic terms is awe-inducing. The timescales of biographical time and human history have come to be dwarfed by what the sciences have revealed of the timescales of geology, evolution and cosmology. The development of modern geology in the early 19th century revealed that what had been thought of as a stable and timeless world of rocks and rivers, hills and valleys, is the product of gradual physical changes taking places over billions of years. This new geological knowledge furnished the framework for evolutionary theory, showing the variety of living species to be similarly a product of small changes and adaptations on a vast timescale. Our understanding of our human origins, far

CONCLUSION

from diminishing us as initial reactions to Darwinian theory supposed, locates us within an amazing story. As Darwin wrote at the end of his *Origin of Species*:

> There is grandeur in this view of life, with its several powers, having been originally breathed into a few forms or into one; and that, whilst this planet has gone cycling on according to the fixed law of gravity, from so simple a beginning endless forms most beautiful and most wonderful have been, and are being, evolved.[8]

The sciences of cosmology in one direction and of quantum physics in the other have subsequently revealed a universe of mind-numbing complexity, of dark matter and black holes, of sub-atomic particles and quantum fields. In the words of Einstein:

> The most beautiful thing we can experience is the mysterious. It is the source of all true art and science. He to whom this emotion is a stranger, who can no longer pause to wonder and stand rapt in awe, is as good as dead: his eyes are closed.[9]

As Einstein says, the mysterious which gives rise to feelings of wonder and awe is evoked not only by the sciences but also by the arts. Whereas the sciences explain our experience with impersonal theories which reveal the world to be vastly different from what we might suppose, the arts can enrich our own individual experience, our perceptions and emotions. Music in all its forms expands and expresses our emotional experience, helping us to recognize the depths and complexities of what we are feeling. The visual arts open our eyes to the variety and beauty of the world around us – the grandeur of a mountain peak or a storm at sea, the play of light and colour on the water or the trees, and the mystery of another human life revealed in a portrait. The literary arts – poems and stories and novels, as well as films and plays – give us a language with which to make sense of our own experience, helping us to realise that we are not alone, that our troubles can be surmounted and our joys can be shared.

Humanism, then, is rooted in the familiar and the ordinary which is at the same time extraordinary. Humanism is a reminder of what is in one sense 'mundane' but is also precious. We do not need to search for some other world, separate from the world in which we live, in order to find inspiration. Above all, humanism draws on the reminder that the actions of people, of so-called 'ordinary people', can be a source of inspiration. I have emphasized that humanism does not idealize human beings, still less 'worship humanity'. But for every tale of human failure, there is a matching story of human resilience, of human solidarity in adversity, of human responses to heartbreak and tragedy, of dedication and determination. A humanism rooted in the one world we share can furnish the beliefs and values enabling us to make the most of the one life we have.

NOTES

Chapter 1

1. Erich Fromm, *The Anatomy of Human Destructiveness* (Holt, Rinehart and Winston, New York, 1973), pp. 230–2, accessed at https://archive.org/details/ErichFrommTheAnatomyOfHumanDestructiveness/mode/2up
2. *British Social Attitudes 36*, edited by John Curtice, Elizabeth Clery, Jane Perry, Miranda Phillips and Nilufer Rahim (National Centre for Social Research, 2019), p. 19, accessed at natcen.ac.uk/publications/british-social-attitudes-36
3. *British Social Attitudes 36*, p. 20.
4. *British Social Attitudes 36*, p. 21.
5. www.pewresearch.org/religion/2021/12/14/about-three-in-ten-u-s-adults-are-now-religiously-unaffiliated/
6. A prominent writer on this subject is the sociologist Steve Bruce. See, for instance, Steve Bruce, *Secularization: In Defence of an Unfashionable Theory* (Oxford University Press, 2011), which includes extensive references to criticisms of the theory.
7. The same word was used by Julian Huxley, another of the pioneers of modern organised humanism, in Julian Huxley (ed.), *The Humanist Frame* (George Allen & Unwin, 1961).
8. M. Rangacarya (ed.), *The Sarva-Siddhanta-Sangraha of Sankaracarya* (Government Press, Madras, 1909), Ch II, p. 5, accessed at www.raoinseattle.com/library/03%20Hinduism/Adi%20Shankara%20Sarva%20Siddhanta%20Sangraha.pdf
9. David Friedrich Strauss, *The Life of Jesus Critically Examined* (SCM Press, 1973), p. 39, accessed at www.gutenberg.org/files/64037/64037-h/64037-h.htm
10. Strauss, p. 88.
11. See Nicolas Walter, *Humanism: What's in the Word* (Rationalist Press Association, 1997), pp. 23–8.

12 George Jacob Holyoake, *English Secularism: A Confession of Belief* (Open Court, 1896), p. 35, accessed at https://archive.org/details/englishsecularis00holyiala/page/n7/mode/2up
13 See Walter, especially pp. 42–78.

Chapter 2

1 The theory is to be found especially in Plato's *Phaedo* and in *The Republic*, Books 5–7. There are many translations and editions, including Plato, *The Last Days of Socrates: Euthyphro, Apology, Crito, Phaedo*, translated by Hugh Tredennick and Harold Tarrant (Penguin Classics, 2003), and Plato, *The Republic*, translated by H.D.P. Lee (Penguin Classics, 2007).
2 The classic text is Descartes's *Meditations*, Second Meditation. Many editions and translations exist, including René Descartes, *Meditations on First Philosophy*, edited and translated by John Cottingham (Cambridge University Press, 2017).
3 Gilbert Ryle, *The Concept of Mind* (Penguin Books, 1963), p. 17 (first published 1949).
4 John 4:24.
5 Miguel de Unamuno, *The Tragic Sense of Life in Men and in Peoples*, translated by J.E. Crawford Flitch (Macmillan and Co., 1921), p. 258, accessed at https://archive.org/details/thetragicsenseof00unamuoft/mode/2up
6 Matthew Arnold, 'Hymn to Empedocles', in Andrew Copson and Alice Roberts (eds), *The Little Book of Humanism* (Little, Brown Book Group, 2020), p. 176.
7 Martin Hägglund, *This Life: Why Mortality Makes Us Free* (Profile Books, 2019), p. 5.
8 Julian Huxley (ed.), *The Humanist Frame* (George Allen & Unwin Ltd, 1961), p. 48.

Chapter 3

1 *British Social Attitudes 36*, edited by John Curtice, Elizabeth Clery, Jane Perry, Miranda Phillips and Nilufer Rahim, 2019, p. 28, accessed at https://natcen.ac.uk/publications/british-social-attitudes-36; Stephen Bullivant, Miguel Farias, Jonathan Lanman and Lois Lee, *Understanding Unbelief: Atheists and Agnostics Around the World* (St Mary's University London, 2019), pp. 13–14, accessed at https://kar.kent.ac.uk/78815/1/Bullivant%20

et%20al%20%282019%29%20Understanding%20Unbelief%20Atheists%20and%20agnostics%20around%20the%20world.pdf
2. Leo Tolstoy, *A Confession* (1882), in *A Confession, The Gospel in Brief, and What I Believe*, translated by Aylmer Maude (Oxford University Press, 1940), pp. 17–18 and 24.
3. A.C. Grayling, 'The Meaning of Life', in *Thinking of Answers: Questions in the Philosophy of Everyday Life* (Bloomsbury, London, 2011), p. 325.
4. Karl Marx, 'Alienated Labour', in *Karl Marx: Selected Writings*, edited by David McLellan (Oxford University Press, 1977), p. 82.
5. Karl Marx, 'Private Property and Communism', in McLellan (ed.), p. 90.
6. A.E. Housman, *A Shropshire Lad*, in *Collected Poems* (Penguin Books, 1956), p. 23.
7. Martin Hägglund, *This Life: Why Mortality Makes Us Free* (Profile Books, 2019), p. 5.

Chapter 4

1. Accessed at www.birmingham.ac.uk/schools/ptr/departments/theologyandreligion/events/cadburylectures/2021/index.aspx
2. www.gov.uk/government/news/guidance-on-promoting-british-values-in-schools-published
3. Erich Fromm, *The Sane Society* (Routledge & Kegan Paul, 1963), Ch 3, pp. 27–66.
4. Fromm, p. 30.
5. Fromm, pp. 36–7.
6. Fromm, p. 38.
7. Fromm, pp. 60–1.

Chapter 5

1. Robin Gill, *Theology in a Social Context* (Routledge, 2012), Ch 10, 'Secularization Re-visited'.
2. John Stuart Mill, *Auguste Comte and Positivism* (N. Trübner & Co, 1866), pp. 153–4, accessed at https://archive.org/details/dli.bengal.10689.4732/mode/2up
3. Gustav Spiller, *The Ethical Movement in Great Britain* (Farleigh Press, 1934), p. 2, accessed at https://archive.org/details/in.ernet.dli.2015.214804/page/n7/mode/2up. See also https://heritage.humanists.uk/the-ethical-movement/ and other resources on the Humanist Heritage website. I am grateful to Madeleine Goodall,

Humanists UK Coordinator of Humanist Heritage, for valuable information and guidance.

[4] Spiller, pp. 61–92, and see also https://heritage.humanists.uk/the-ethical-church/

[5] Robert N. Bellah, Richard Madsen, William M. Sullivan, Ann Swidler and Steven M. Tipton, *Habits of the Heart* (University of California Press, 1985, reprinted 2008).

[6] Bellah et al, p. 219.

[7] Bellah et al, p. 222.

[8] Bellah et al, p. 230.

[9] Robert D. Putnam, *Bowling Alone* (Simon & Schuster, 2000).

[10] Putnam, p. 19.

[11] Putnam, p. 66.

[12] Putnam, p. 361.

[13] Roberta Katz, Sarah Ogilvie, Jane Shaw and Linda Woodhead, *Gen Z, Explained* (University of Chicago Press, 2021), p. 122.

Chapter 6

[1] Thomas Paine, *Political Writings* (Cambridge University Press, 1989), pp. 207–8.

[2] Paine, p. 228.

[3] Paine, p. 221.

[4] Paine, pp. 211 and 212.

[5] Paine, p. 242.

[6] Paine, p. 77.

[7] Paine, p. 166.

[8] William Godwin, *Memoirs of Wollstonecraft* (Woodstock Books, 1993), pp. 33–4.

[9] Mary Wollstonecraft, *The Rights of Woman* (Dent, 1970), p. 15.

[10] Wollstonecraft, p. 59.

[11] Wollstonecraft, p. 61.

[12] *The Republican*, Vol. 1, No. 2, 3 September 1819, p. 21, accessed at https://archive.org/details/republican00carl/mode/2up

[13] Richard Carlile, *An Address to Men of Science*, Printed and published by R. Carlile, 55, Fleet Street, 1821, pp. 17–18. Accessed at https://archive.org/details/anaddresstomens00carlgoog

[14] John Stuart Mill, 'The Utility of Religion', in *Three Essays on Religion* (Prometheus Books, 1998), p. 110.

[15] John Stuart Mill, 'On Liberty', in *Utilitarianism*, edited by Mary Warnock (Fontana, 1962), p. 136.

[16] Mill, 'On Liberty', p. 187.

NOTES

17 Mill, 'On Liberty', pp. 185 and 187.
18 John Stuart Mill, *Utilitarianism, Liberty, and Representative Government*, edited by H.B. Acton (Dent, 1972), p. 216.
19 John Stuart Mill and Harriet Taylor Mill, *Essays on Sex Equality* (University of Chicago Press, 1970), p. 236.
20 https://humanists.international/what-is-humanism/the-amsterdam-declaration/
21 Bertrand Russell, *The Practice and Theory of Bolshevism* (George Allen and Unwin, 1920), p. 8.
22 Erich Fromm (ed.), *Socialist Humanism: An International Symposium* (Doubleday, 1965). See especially Fromm's Introduction. Accessed at https://files.libcom.org/files/Socialist%20Humanism.pdf
23 An outspoken advocate of such a position was the humanist philosopher Antony Flew. See, for example, Antony Flew, *The Politics of Procrustes* (Temple Smith, 1981). A piece written specifically for a humanist readership is Antony Flew, 'Prophets of the Procrustean Collective', in *Free Inquiry* at https://secularhumanism.org/1981/04/prophets-of-the-procrustean-collective/
24 A powerful case for greater equality is to be found in the work of Kate Pickett and Richard Wilkinson. Pickett is a Patron of Humanists UK. See, for example, Richard Wilkinson and Kate Pickett, *The Spirit Level* (Allen Lane, 2009).
25 Huxley was a prominent member of the Eugenics Society in the 1930s, and its president in 1959–62. He insisted that the measures which he and the Society advocated were in total contrast to the 'crazy mentality' of the Nazi eugenics programme and its ideas of racial superiority. He advocated the use of sterilization to prevent the passing on of 'mental disorders' to the next generation, and it was voluntary, not compulsory, sterilization that he proposed – but it seems that his rejection of the latter was not unequivocal. He also coined the term 'transhumanism' to refer to his belief that, by means of biotechnology, 'The human species can, if it wishes, transcend itself – not just sporadically, an individual here in one way, an individual there in another way, but in its entirety, as humanity.' Such ideas could be seen to be at odds with his humanism. See Alison Bashford, *An Intimate History of Evolution: The Story of the Huxley Family* (Penguin Books, 2023), Ch 9, especially pp. 347–51 and 356–8.
26 Bashford, pp. 183–96.

Chapter 7

1. Yuval Noah Harari, *Homo Deus* (Vintage, Penguin Random House, 2017), p. 259.
2. John Gray, *Seven Types of Atheism* (Penguin Books, 2019), p. 24.
3. Gray, p. 25.
4. Gray, p. 31.
5. These words were subsequently incorporated into a joint statement agreed by Russell and Albert Einstein and released in July 1955, which came to be known as the Russell-Einstein Manifesto. See https://dearbertie.mcmaster.ca/letter/einstein#:~:text=In%20the%20 1950s%2C%20Bertrand%20Russell,to%20do%20something%20 about%20it
6. John Stuart Mill, *Utilitarianism*, edited by Mary Warnock (Fontana, Collins, 1962), pp. 265–6.
7. As mentioned in Chapter 6, note 25, the term 'transhumanism' was coined by Julian Huxley in 1957. He hoped that it might serve to refer to the idea of 'man remaining man, but transcending himself, by realizing new possibilities of and for his human nature' (Alison Bashford, *An Intimate History of Evolution: The Story of the Huxley Family*, Penguin Books, 2023, p. 356). As a proponent of evolutionary humanism, Huxley supposed that the evolutionary process would continue, but was vague about how this could be promoted. His term has acquired other and more radical connotations since then.
8. Charles Darwin, *The Origin of Species*, 1st edition (John Murray, 1859), p. 490, accessed at https://archive.org/details/onoriginofspec00darw
9. Albert Einstein, 'What I Believe', *Forum and Century*, Vol. 84, No. 4, October 1930, pp. 193–4, accessed at https://archive.org/details/sim_forum-and-century_1930-10_84_4

FURTHER READING

A comprehensive coverage of humanism in its various aspects, historical and contemporary, and with multiple pointers to further reading, is:

Andrew Copson and A.C. Grayling (eds.), *The Wiley Blackwell Handbook of Humanism* (John Wiley & Sons Ltd., 2015).

A more thorough presentation and defence in depth of the view of humanism put forward in the present book can be found in:

Andrew Copson, Luke Donnellan and Richard Norman, *Understanding Humanism* (Routledge, 2022).

Two concise introductions are:

Stephen Law, *Humanism: A Very Short Introduction* (Oxford University Press, 2011).
Peter Cave, *Humanism: A Beginner's Guide* (Oneworld Publications, 2009, new edition 2022).

A very readable and practical presentation of humanism in a US context is:

Greg M. Epstein, *Good Without God: What a Billion Nonreligious People Do Believe* (Harper, 2010).

Also from a North American perspective, an optimistic view of the relation between humanism and the possibility of human progress, based on the historical record, is:

Steven Pinker, *Enlightenment Now: The Case for Reason, Science, Humanism and Progress* (Penguin Books, 2018).

On secularization and the debate around it, referred to in Chapter 1, Steve Bruce has written extensively. For his defence of the thesis, and his response to criticisms, see:

Steve Bruce, *Secularization: In Defence of an Unfashionable Theory* (Oxford University Press, 2011).

A clear introduction to the case for naturalism and its implications for the rejection of belief in God or gods, as discussed in Chapter 2, is:

Julian Baggini, *Atheism: A Very Short Introduction* (Oxford University Press, 2003, new edition 2021).

The historical tradition
An engaging survey of the humanist tradition, understood in a broad sense, is:

Sarah Bakewell, *Humanly Possible* (Chatto & Windus, 2023).

A classic text from the ancient world is Lucretius' *On the Nature of Things*. There are various translations, including:

Lucretius, *The Nature of Things*, translated by A.E. Stallings (Penguin Classics, 2007).

An earlier and very readable prose translation, now out of print, is:

Lucretius, *On the Nature of the Universe*, translated by Ronald Latham (Penguin Classics, 1974).

The place of the 18th-century European Enlightenment in the humanist tradition is epitomized in the writings of David Hume and his ironic style of religious scepticism. A representative selection is conveniently collected in:

Hume on Religion, edited by Julian Baggini (The Philosophy Press, 2010).

As examples of the interplay between the humanist tradition and political movements discussed in Chapter 6, some readily available texts are:

Thomas Paine, *Political Writings*, edited by Bruce Kuklick (Cambridge University Press, 1989). (This edition includes both parts of *The Rights of Man*, and the first part of *The Age of Reason*.)
Mary Wollstonecraft, *A Vindication of the Rights of Woman* (Penguin Classics, 2004).

The most important of John Stuart Mill's philosophical and political writings are readily accessible. Two of his works most congenial to a humanist perspective are in:

John Stuart Mill, *On Liberty and The Subjection of Women* (Penguin Classics, 2006).

Online resources
Two invaluable websites, both under the auspices of Humanists UK, are:

Humanist Heritage – a rich collection of material exploring the history of humanism in the UK: https://heritage.humanists.uk/

Understanding Humanism – a resource aimed especially at schools, teachers and students but useful for anyone wanting to learn more about humanism: https://understandinghumanism.org.uk/

More about the international humanist movement can be found on the Humanists International website at:

https://humanists.international/what-is-humanism/

INDEX

A
Adler, Felix 24, 92
agnosticism 23
Aquinas 13
Aristotle 34
Arnold, Matthew 22, 45
artificial intelligence 132–5
arts 137–8
assisted dying 83
atheism 39–42
authenticity 53–4
autonomy 83
Averroes 13

B
Baggini, Julian 146
Bakewell, Sarah 146
Bashford, Alison 143
beliefs ch. 2 *passim*
Bellah, Robert 96–7
belonging 89–90, 100–3
Besant, Annie 114, 120
biotechnology 132
Bradlaugh, Charles 24, 114
British Humanist Association 24, 94
Bruce, Steve 139, 146
Buddhism 11

C
Carlile, Richard 111–14
Cave, Peter 145
Chavarkas 17
Christianity 6–10, 94–5, 99–100
churches 95–100
climate change 124
Coit, Stanton 94
communism 120–1
community 57–8, 74–7, ch. 5 *passim*
compassion 80, 83
Comte, Auguste 91–2, 114
contraception 114
Conway Hall 93
Conway, Moncure 93
Copson, Andrew 145
cosmology 136–7
creativity 54–6

D
Darwin, Charles 20–22, 137
death 16–17, 43–6, 49–50, 56, 61–4, 132–3
deism 18–19, 105–7
democracy 109, 116–18, 135
Democritus 15
Descartes, René 35–6
D'Holbach, Baron 19
digital technology 102–3, 132–5
Donnellan, Luke 145
dualism 33–9

E
economic inequality 120–2
Einstein, Albert 137
Eliot, George 22–3

empathy 77–8
Empedocles 15
Enlightenment 18–19, 104–5
environmentalism 123–5
Epicurus 16, 44
Epstein, Greg M. 145
equality 105–11, 118–23
ethical societies 24, 92–4, 120
eugenics 124, 143
evolution 21, 29, 124, 136–7
evolutionary psychology 31–2

F

facts and values 69–76
fairness 79
Feuerbach, Ludwig 22–3
Flew, Antony 143
folk psychology 32
frame, framework (of orientation and devotion) 1–5, 11, 27, 46–7, 48, 65, 87, 126
freedom 105, 114–19
freedom of religion and belief 105
freedom of speech and expression 105, 112, 115
free-thinkers 18
French Revolution 105, 107–8
Freud, Sigmund 59
Fromm, Erich 2–3, 65, 72–6, 121–2, 126
funerals, humanist 62–3, 95
future generations 56–8, 124

G

gay sexuality, gay rights 86, 119
geology 21, 29, 136
Gen Z 102
Gill, Robin 89
God, gods 11–12, 39–42
Godwin, William 108–9
Greece 14–16

H

happiness 115, 117, 131
Hägglund, Martin 46, 60
Hinduism 9, 17, 100
Holyoake, George 23
honesty 78–9
Housman, A.E. 60
'humanist', 'humanism', use of the words 18, 22, 24–5, 55, 123
humanist ceremonies (weddings, funerals) 95
Humanists International 25
Humanists UK 24, 94–5
Hume, David 19, 147
Huxley, Julian 47, 124–5, 127, 139, 143
Huxley, T.H. 22

I

India 16–17
inspiration 138
International Humanist and Ethical Union 25
Islam 6, 9–10, 100

K

kindness 80
King, Martin Luther 99

L

Law, Steven 145
Leucippus 15
literature 138
Lokayata 17
loyalty 79–80
Lucretius 16, 44, 146–7
Lyell, Charles 21

M

Maimonides 13
Marx, Karl 22, 55, 121
materialism 28
mathematics 34

INDEX

meaning 46–7, ch. 3 *passim*
Mill, John Stuart 92, 114–18, 127, 129–31, 147
mind 35–9
miracles 19–21
morality 76–7, 83–7
music 137–8

N

naturalism 14–19, ch. 2 *passim*, 126, 135
nature, the natural world 58–60
needs 1–5, 71–7, 103
neuroscience 31–2
nuclear war 131–2

P

Paine, Thomas 18–19, 105–11, 147
Peterloo Massacre 111–13
physicalism 28
Pickett, Kate 143
Pinker, Steven 146
Plato 33–4
politics ch. 6 *passim*, 127
posthumanism 132–5
progress 129–32
purpose 48–9
Putnam, Robert 97–9

R

racial equality 119
rationalists 18
reason 12–14, 110
reductionism 30–2
religion 5–13, 39–43, 67–9, 85–8, 89–91, 127–9
religion of humanity 91–2, 114–15, 127
Renaissance 18
rights, human 105, 110–11
Ruge, Arnold 22

Russell, Bertrand 120–1, 129, 131
Ryle, Gilbert 37–8

S

Santayana, George 47
science 13–14, 28–32, 46, 136–7
secularists, secularism 18, 23–4
secularization 9–10
social capital 96–9
socialism 120–2
soul 35, 43
spirit 39, 41
spiritual, spirituality 30, 39, 47
stories 61–4, 138
Strauss, David Friedrich 20–23
supernatural 28, 33, 41

T

Taoism 11
Taylor, Harriet 118
Tolstoy, Leo 49–50, 56
tragedy 44–5
transhumanism 132–5, 143–4

U

Unamuno, Miguel de 43–4
Unitarians 94–5
Utilitarianism, utility 115, 117, 130

V

values 33–4, ch. 4 *passim*, 91, 127, 134–5
Voltaire 19

W

Walter, Nicolas 139
Ward, Mrs Humphry 21
weddings, humanist 95–6
Wilkinson, Richard 143
Wollstonecraft, Mary 108–11, 147
women's rights 110–11, 114, 118
Woodhead, Linda 67
worldview 11

www.ingramcontent.com/pod-product-compliance
Lightning Source LLC
Chambersburg PA
CBHW020416080526
44584CB00014B/1364